Stand Tall

AGAINST THE ODDS

Everett W. Rau
as told to Laura Shore

*"While we live, our bodies are moving particles
of earth, joined inextricably both to the soil
and to the bodies of other living creatures.
It is hardly surprising, then, that there should be
some profound resemblances between
our treatment of our bodies and our treatment
of the earth."*

Wendell Berry, The Unsettling of America
Quoted by Daphne Miller, MD, Farmacology

To GOOD FOLKS

E. Rau

2016

Stand Tall

AGAINST THE ODDS

The Improbable Journey of
an American Farmer

Everett W. Rau
as told to Laura Shore

Farm Share Studio Press
Altamont, New York
2015

Many thanks to Keith Lee, Don Shore, Margaret Shore, Robert Shore, Barbara Harris, Nancy Ota, and Marijo Dougherty for their encouragement and contributions to early drafts.

Thanks to Ken Rau for the fantastic photos of family and Pleasant View Farm — especially the documentation of building the barn.

And thanks to Ev and Peg Rau for their stories.

Farm Share Studio Press
P.O. Box 433
Altamont, New York 12009
www.farmsharestudio.com
farmsharestudio@gmail.com

Printed in the United States of America
ISBN 9781517082529

First edition

Contents

Left: Photo of Everett Rau taken by Viola Gray in 1923.
Right: Everett at 95 taken by Laura Shore in 2014.

Preface

I have wanted to write a book about my life for a long time. But as a farm boy, who barely made it out of high school, I hardly dreamed it would happen. Then one day in 2014 I got a call from Marijo Dougherty, Curator of the Altamont Archives and Museum. Would I like to participate in a public interview on my life in farming to coincide with an exhibit they were doing on the Altamont Fair? At 95, I had learned a thing or two about farming and life. And though I have spoken in historical societies across the region about Dutch Barns and antique farm tools, I had never before spoken in my home town of Altamont.

Marijo introduced me to my interviewer, Laura Shore, and over the next few weeks we met at the kitchen table and she helped me stir up memories of early farming and talk about how the old ways connect with my vision for the future of our family farm. When the big day came, I could hardly believe that the Altamont Village Hall was full of so many friendly faces. Seeing so many people I knew was like rocket fuel and I talked without stopping for over an hour. I never expected a standing ovation. It was so touching.

This is my story. It's the story of my early life as a farm boy, ashamed to be with people outside my family circle, and unable to be the person I wanted to be. It's a story of fear, anger, hard work, success in business, total failure, and finally true success as I dedicated my life to helping people understand the good old way that people lived and worked out life's problems. I hope something in this book will help someone (maybe you) to keep on trying and never give up so that you will be able to join me in standing tall against the odds of life.

Everett W. Rau
October 2015

Ev's Grandparents
Sarah Frederick: 1847–1917
Peter J. Ogsbury: 1843–1928
    Married: 1868
        Elizabeth (Libbie): 1870–1935
        Clayton: 1873–1958
        Margaret: 1880–1962
        Willard: 1882–1963

Ev's Parents
Margaret Van Valkenburg Ogsbury Rau: 1880–1962
Frank Emil Rau: 1873–1954
    Married: 1902
        Two died as infants
        Ernest Rau: 1904–1928
        Raymond Rau: 1906–1973
        Clayton Rau: 1908–1913
        Edward Rau: 1917–1924
        Everett Rau: 1919
            Married Margaret Vedder b.1923 in 1943
                Jim: 1944
                Mary Jane: 1947
                Ernie: 1949
                Ken: 1957

Introduction

It's the week before Memorial Day, 2015. Ev Rau and I are sitting across from each other at a folding table in the cluttered parlor of his Federal-style farm house. In addition to the piles of dusty farming journals, newsletters, and health magazines, we've added new piles of photo albums and boxes of loose snapshots. I look over guiltily at his wife, Peg, who is focused on her iPad and trying to ignore the new addition to the clutter. Peg is 92, and though she has recovered from congestive heart failure and broken hips, her mobility is very limited. Ev, who is 95, tends to meals, housework and caregiving. His spine is curved like the letter C and he recently admitted, sheepishly, that he's beginning to slow down a bit.

The window is open to a lively cross breeze and I can see the Green mountains of Vermont as I gaze across the fields of Pleasant View Farm, which slope down in the east toward Albany. The room is quiet when Ev hands me an antique metal box. I look up quizzically into his bright, brown eyes, and when I open it, I see that this is where his mother saved her precious keepsakes. There's a lock of her sister's hair, along with Christmas cards in flowery script from favorite farm customers and summer boarders. There are telegrams from her son Ernest, as he traveled, in the year he would die.

This intimate excavation is the result of a year-long conversation with Ev and Peg that began with a public interview I conducted for the Altamont Archives. Growing old today in America is no longer the achievement that it once was. But those who know Ev continue to be inspired by the twists and turns his life has taken and his ability to grow and change and conceive ambitious new projects well into his nineties. We began by discussing the plans he was hatching with his son, Ken, and grandson, Tim, to restart the family farm along the lines of ecological farming I had read about in Michael Pollan's book, *The Omnivore's Dilemma*. When Ev said he wanted to write a book, I thought we were writing a book about farming and readily agreed. I was excited to talk with someone who grew up when people still farmed with horses and it was fun to have him answer my naïve farming questions with the patience and clarity of a born teacher.

It quickly became clear to me that our book would not be about farming, exactly, but about Ev's life in a more complete way. For over a year we met each Tuesday morning for about two hours with a tape recorder. During the week Ev jotted new notes and phrases in a little black and white composition notebook and small yellow legal pads, while I transcribed the recordings, worked to shape a coherent narrative, and tried to pin down fuzzy recollections through research. In the end I chose to tell Ev and Peg's story using their own words, where possible. My contribution has been to take the jumble of memories and string them together like beads in time. I've also used research to help clarify memories and to recover the history of Peg's family. By researching the life of Ev's father I was able to transform him from a childhood bogeyman to real human being and allow Ev to see him for the first time as a gifted but troubled man.

We live in a golden age of genealogical research. The entire *Altamont Enterprise* is searchable on line, as is the *Schenectady Gazette*. But though genealogy sites abound with answers, nothing can take the place of finding time to sit and talk with the elders in our lives and really listen to the truths embedded in their stories.

Laura Shore
Farm Share Studio Press
Altamont, New York

Stand Tall

AGAINST THE ODDS

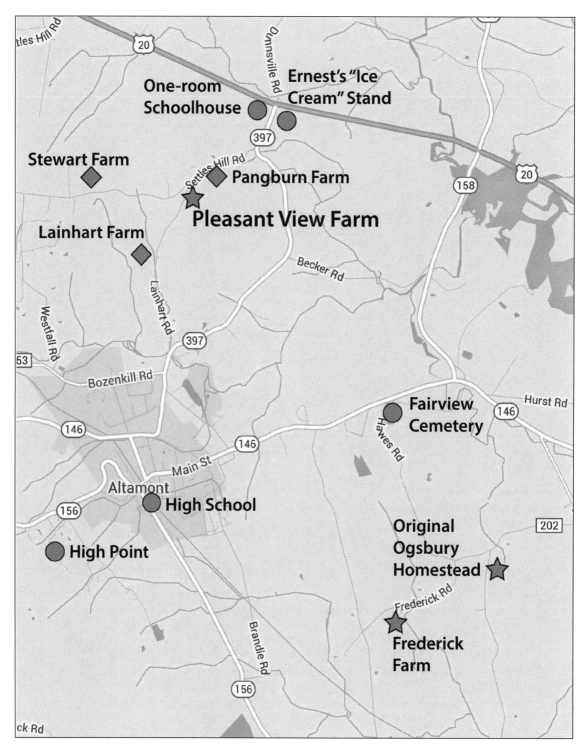

Landmarks from Ev's life in Altamont, Guilderland, and Dunnsville.

Chapter 1

Pleasant View Farm

Everett Rau's family has lived on Pleasant View Farm since the early 1800s. The farm sits on 130 acres of hilly land at the intersection of Settles Hill and Lainhart Roads on a steep slope overlooking the Albany-county town of Guilderland, New York. The farm was part of a crossroads community called Dunnsville, at the intersection of the Great Western Turnpike (now Route 20) and Route 397. At the turn of the century, Dunnsville had a post office, a one-room schoolhouse, a wayside inn, and general store. What follows is Ev's story.

My grandfather, Peter Ogsbury, was born in 1843 and his daily patterns of life were not unlike my own when I was growing up. Life on Pleasant View Farm revolved around the seasons. In Grandfather's day there were twelve cows for milk, six pigs, five horses and any number of chickens. Corn, oats, buckwheat, barley, wheat, rye, and hay for straw were grown for sale and for animal feed. In spring the fruit trees needed to be cared for, including pruning and renewing the trees by grafting scions onto mature stems. Vegetable gardens provided summer food and winter preserves. Plowing was done by a two-horse plow that one man would walk behind. In the fall, two or three teams would rotate through the neighboring farms, working together during threshing, and butchering. They put in long hours but created a festive atmosphere that made the work go by quickly.

When they were growing up in the 1880s my mother, Margaret Ogsbury, her sister Libbie and her brothers Clayton and Willard ran across plowed fields and wooded lots, still towering with old-growth pines, maples, hickory nut, and hemlock trees. If Mother stopped in the shade of the Dutch barn while collecting eggs from the chickens that ran wild in the yard, she could have looked across open fields all the way to South Schenectady in the north and Albany in the east – as well as Mt. Greylock and Mt. Equinox in the Berkshires. On a cold winter morning she could see the plumes of wood smoke rising from kitchen chimneys on the many neighboring farms in the Dunnsville area – the Wagners, the Livingstons, Van Wormers, Crounses, Kemners, and Pangburns. She would laugh with her family to hear pious old Aaron Pangburn's bible hymns being punctuated with "Damn the farm!" when he hit a rock while plowing – followed shortly with more bible hymns.

They studied at the one-room Dunnsville school where their mother, Sarah Ogsbury, was the teacher. They lived in a two-story Federal-style house that was quite modern for its time, with a new hand pump in the kitchen designed to let water out of the pump

on freezing nights, to be primed in the morning with warm water from the reservoir of the cook stove. The kitchen was the heart of the house, especially in winter, with its large black-iron wood-fired cook stove, which was heated many more hours a day than the parlor stove. On long winter evenings the family gathered around the kitchen table, lit by a kerosene lamp, to talk about the next day's work, read the bible, and do small tasks.

Family

My Ogsbury ancestors descended from David Auxburger, who traveled from Switzerland in 1765 and eventually fought in the American Revolution. You can still see his original house, set back from Depot Road, in Guilderland. Though the house is still there, his old Dutch barn has been moved to the Philipsburg Manor historic site in Sleepy Hollow, NY. Grandfather Peter J. Ogsbury, was born at Pleasant View Farm, and served with distinction in the Civil War. Upon returning, he courted Sarah Amanda Frederick, whose family lived on a farm in the Meadowdale area, near the original Ogsbury homestead. Sarah had attended local schools and then the Lutheran Hartwick Seminary (now Hartwick College) where she was trained to teach in district public schools. Once married, she moved to her new husband's homestead and taught in the one room schoolhouse in nearby Dunnsville. About then, one neighbor, Stephen Lainhart, married her sister Mary Magdalene Frederick and another, Aaron Fuller Pangburn, married the third sister, Martha Frederick. It was Stephen Lainhart, along with many neighbors, who helped my grandfather move a Dutch barn from the Aaron Pangburn farm to his own. Together they were to form a tight knit group that helped each other out during harvest time and kept each other company in the quiet corner of western Guilderland.

My mother was one of four children. Her older sister, Libbie, married J. Kaley Wemple and moved to Schenectady where they "farmed" a double lot in Niskayuna and Kaley was a maintenance superintendent of the high school. Her brother Clayton married Margaret Shoudy and also moved to Schenectady where they had a home on Parkwood Boulevard. Her youngest brother, Willard, stayed in Altamont and worked on and off the farm for many years and taught me much about farming. In fact, he lived on the farm while I was in high school when his marriage to Blanche Strevell didn't work out.

Ogsbury family
Top row: Clayton Ogsbury, Kaley Wemple, Everett Wemple, Frank Rau, Willard Ogsbury.
Middle row: Margaret Ogsbury (Clayton's wife), Libbie Ogsbury Wemple, Sarah Ogsbury, Peter J. Ogsbury, Margaret Ogsbury Rau, Blanche Ogsbury (wife of Willard).
Front row: Eleanor Ogsbury, Kenneth Wemple, Ernest Rau, Raymond Rau and Willard's daughters, Mildred and Dorothy Ogsbury.

The Rau family and friends in Schenectady at 133 Fairview before moving to the farm. Note the sign in the window below reads Furnished Rooms.

The boys in both photos are Raymond (left) and Ernest (right). The women in the large hats are probably Frederick relatives.

Mother was 19 when she met my father. He was, in many ways, a tall dark-haired hand-some stranger. An artist, the son of German immigrants, Frank Emil Rau was seven years older than she and could not have been more different than the people she had known all her life. His parents married in Germany before they set off for America on the passenger ship Bremen in 1869. They settled first in Schenectady and then in Syracuse. My grand-father Rau worked as a gardener, but died in 1886. My father then left school after eighth grade to work with his three brothers to support their widowed mother. The family lived in a comfortable three-story shingled house, which let rooms for boarders.

I never learned how my parents met, but a brief notice in the *Altamont Enterprise* reported in 1900 that "*Frank E. Rau who has been spending several months as an atten-dant in one of the Brooklyn hospitals, has returned here and is spending a few days at Peter J. Ogsbury's farm near Dunnsville.*" The 1900 census does find him in a Greenwich Village boarding house, where he listed his profession as an artist. There was an art exhibition of the Brooklyn YMCA Sketch Club that included work by Frank E. Rau. By 1902 he had moved to 17 Western Avenue, a pleasant Albany neighborhood near Washington Park, and was working as decorator. According to the *Enterprise*, this is where he and Mother went after their "quiet but pretty house wedding" on April 30, 1902. In 1903 they moved to Harrison Avenue in Schenectady, where he worked as a horse-team driver before taking a job at General Electric as a commercial artist, drawing line pictures that engravers would reproduce for printed manuals and catalogs. Eventually they moved into a nicer house on Fairview Avenue in the Bellevue section of town.

My parents had seven children, but only Ernest, Raymond, and I lived to adult-hood. The family traveled frequently back and forth between Schenectady and Pleasant View Farm, participating in Ogsbury family reunions and other social events. My grand-mother Sarah's health began to decline when she was in her eighties and Mother spent more time at the farm. When she died in 1917, my father gave up his G.E. job and moved to the farm with Mother and their boys.

For Mother, moving back to the farm must have felt like putting on comfortable well-worn shoes. She had grown up with the rhythms of farming – cooking for big appe-tites, putting up foods for winter, and gardening. I expect that she quickly adapted to the challenges of managing the house. But most of all, she enjoyed the sense of belonging that washed over her every Sunday during services at St. John's Lutheran – a church that the Ogsbury family had helped establish in 1872 just eight years before she was born. Though still a small village, Altamont was an important rail station for the rural train lines and seemed an up and coming place. Grandfather was a town auditor and her uncle John Ogsbury was editor of the *Altamont Enterprise*. Yet I believe that as much as she enjoyed socializing with friends in town, she loved being on the land, surrounded by her flower gardens. Hilltop farms may be challenging for farmers but the open landscape provides long views that can lift your spirit and make your heart sing.

From what I heard growing up, my father detested the farm and made no secret of his bitter feelings. He was not born to farming and though Grandfather and Uncle Will worked hard to teach him, Dad carried on throughout the years with misery and resentment directed mostly toward my mother. From my perspective after all these years, I can see how hard he must have worked to perfect his artistic talent, against all odds. I know he loved his job at General Electric and was happy to make a living using his skills. He and mother were moving up quickly in Schenectady and were comfortable with modern conveniences and new friends. Father was always rigid and he found the distractions of married life and children unsettling. Now he had moved from professional man to hilltop farmer and felt trapped on a godforsaken piece of land in the middle of nowhere, without plumbing or electricity. Six miles might have been 100 if you had to commute by horse and wagon. It was almost worse that you could see Schenectady from the hilltop. It just reinforced his sense of isolation.

Neighbors

Coming from Schenectady, my parents saw an opportunity for selling farm produce in their old neighborhood. They would load up their wagon in summer and bobsleigh in winter and travel over Giffords Church Road or Route 158 to the city. There they would deliver eggs, milk, cottage cheese, butter, fruits and vegetables to residents of the G.E. Plot and housewives in the well-heeled Bellevue neighborhood on the hill above the sprawling G.E. factory complex. At the end of the day Mother would stop for tea with old friends before she and my father headed back to Pleasant View Farm.

The weekly trip to Schenectady by horse and wagon would take the better part of a day and would end with a trip to Mohican Market on Jay Street to deliver any unsold eggs and produce for store credit, which they would use for necessary groceries. Mother liked making the trip in summer, listening to the horse clop along the gravel roads and watching the swallows swoop and dive after insects in the waning light. Winter was a lot more challenging. With only eggs and butter to deliver, the route was less profitable and it could be bitterly cold. Before setting out, Mother would heat up a piece of soapstone on the iron cook stove and place it under the lap blanket to keep warm. Still, with open fields all around, the roads were often drifted over and with the days so short, it could sometimes be a challenge to find your way back home. These were times when Father would become especially surly. It would take all her energy to keep silent and avoid his wrath.

One winter evening they got started for home later than usual and darkness seemed to fall more quickly. In those days, there were only a few farms on Route 158 in the area between the railroad tracks and Parkers Corners, with no more than four or five houses in a three-mile stretch. It had snowed all day and the wind was drifting snow across the roads and fields – close to whiteout conditions. Farmers in rural areas knew there would be some horse traffic so they would take their kerosene lamp off the kitchen table and put it in the window to help people find their way. About halfway home a gust of wind came across the fields and blew out the two lanterns in the bobsleigh. Cursing, Father tried to light the lamps but in 35 mph wind it was impossible. Fortunately, they could see a dimly lighted window in the distance. Dad was able to take his lanterns into the farmhouse, get them lighted and continue home.

View of Pleasant View Farm from the top of the orchard looking east. Circa 1915.

Top: Eddie and Ev (left) as toddlers.

Lower left: Everett and Rex (over the years all the dogs were named Rex).

Lower right: Mother with Ev as an infant, Father, Grandfather, Raymond, Ernest, and Eddie.

Chapter 2

And So I Begin

I was born on August 22, 1919. World War I had ended and Prohibition would take effect the following year. Women still did not have the vote, but none of that seemed to matter on the farm. Mother was nearly forty. My birth had been difficult and left her with some lasting health problems. I was a frail kid in a frail family fighting to hold onto traditions and keep itself together. Grandfather Ogsbury was 76 and was aided on the farm by my uncle Willard, by my recalcitrant father, and neighboring kin.

My brothers Ernest and Raymond were 15 and 13, and growing fast. Eddie was two years older than me and there are pictures of us together as toddlers. Unfortunately Eddie died of polio when he was seven. I remember standing outside as they carried his limp body out into the yard to get some fresh air. After that, I mostly stayed to myself, with a rock and a bent nail that I kept in my pocket and fondled in my hand for companionship. Except for the summer boarders there was so little conversation in our house that my memories of those years are like snapshots without captions.

The one bright spot was my aunt Libbie, whose soothing voice and thoughtful gifts made me feel a little less alone. She had lost her son Everett to the influenza epidemic the year I was born and suggested that my mother change my name from James Everett to his name, Everett Wemple. Bearing his name made me feel closer to my aunt, though it did create a challenge later when I went to get a driver's license and had to go through a legal process to change my name officially.

I was eight before I went to school. I had a series of ear infections, throat infections, and chest problems. Mother had a big woolen cloth that she would smear with something. She heated it, nearly scalded me to death, then put me to bed. I survived, but school was a long walk down a steep hill and she had me wait until I was strong enough. The delay was fine with me. I had retreated into my own silent world. My parents were consumed by their drama and pretty much ignored me. The only loving touch I recall growing up was when mother would line chairs up near the kitchen stove and drape them with blankets. I would stand in a tub of warm water between the stove and this screen and she would wash me. Before too long she gave me the washcloth and said it was time I washed myself.

As I grew older I would gauge the tension in the house by my mother's silence. Was she humming while she rolled out piecrust or peeled peaches for preserves? Or was she tense and brittle, snapping at me when I made too much noise chasing the cat around the kitchen? In later years my wife Peg would say that the farm seemed to have an invisible line that ran between the barns and the house. The house and gardens made up my mother's world and the men inhabited the rest. During the day my parents could avoid each other, coming together for meals, which were consumed with silent intensity. It was in the evenings that their irritation would flare. My father often badgered Mother with ugly insults, hectoring her as she crossed the yard.

In one memorable moment, when I was very young, he crossed the line and hit her face and broke her glasses. Even now, as a I cross the threshold to the kitchen, I can see the steel-cut picture of her smashed glasses and I still remember the screaming sound of my own voice and the bruising on her face where the glasses had been. It would be a long time before I could stand up to my father. Finally, when I was about fourteen, Father was berating Mother, and she turned to me, saying that his father used to misuse his mother – at which point I looked at Father and said, "Dad it's about time this stopped." And though the abuse abated, my parents rarely spoke more than necessary to each other and the memories of his misbehavior filled me with shame and anger for many years after he died.

Above: Harrowing with our horse, Star. From left to right: Grandfather Ogsbury, Father, Ernest, Raymond and Uncle Willard. *Top facing page:* A good crop of oats drying and waiting for threshing day.

First Farming

By 1920 the German threshing barn, where we kept the cows, was deteriorating and there was no money to fix it. As the condition worsened, Dad started selling off the cows and moved toward raising chickens for eggs and broilers. I'm sure Grandfather hated seeing his years of hard work decline but he was powerless in his old age to reverse it. What little money there was went into a coffee can in the kitchen cabinet to pay for taxes and the things we couldn't grow.

Back then every field had a name, because you had a hired hand. You'd say, "Go and plow the Back lot, or Uncle John's lot, or the Quarry lot." The Hogback lot got its name because the land was curved like the back of a hog. One August, around my eighth birthday, Dad was getting in hay on Uncle John's lot. Thinking back now, it was way too late to get in hay and the quality of the hay was not that great. My father worked grudgingly but he had the farming instinct. He knew the winter would be cold and the one cow and two horses we had left would need food. This would be the last winter for that cow. She was around 14 years old and no longer gave milk. The next fall I can still see my dad putting large pumpkins into the manger in front of the cow and with a flat shovel chopping them into pieces. He then put a couple of quarts of whole ground corn meal on the chopped pumpkin. When I asked him why pumpkins, he answered, "We are fattening the cow and when she stops eating the corn and pumpkins, which she likes very well – the next day we will butcher her."

She stayed in the barnyard in the fall so her muscles would soften – same as you and me if we don't exercise. If you were to eat steak from a non-fattened cow it would have no marbling and be tough. I don't recall that this meat was tender – I'm sure it was tougher than today. A lot would have gone into soups and stews and if you're hungry, with a good set of teeth, you manage pretty well. That was the end of the cows. We got raw milk year round from Johnny Armstrong who had been delivering milk for our summer boarders. We didn't get cows again until after Peggy and I married in June 1943.

Ice Cream

On August 22, 1927, my eighth birthday, I walked with my father down to the icehouse, where we kept blocks of ice, carefully put there in the cold days of winter, covered deeply with sawdust. Almost miraculously, the ice would stay frozen until the cool weather of fall. Dad shoveled some sawdust away and brought out a cake of ice, all dirty with sawdust on it. We took it to the well and hand-pumped a pail of water. This we splashed on the ice, which, to my amazement, became totally clean.

When we brought the ice over to the house, my mother had mixed up fresh peaches, thick cream, eggs, and sugar. We cracked the ice and packed it around the cylinder of a hand-crank ice cream machine. When we put rock salt on top of the ice it started to melt. In high school I would learn that it takes heat for ice to melt and that in this case the salt kept the icy slush cold enough to freeze the ice cream mix. But for me, at eight, this was the first experience that caused me to try to puzzle out how something worked – how on a hot August day, when they stopped turning the crank, the cylinder contained frozen ice cream – which we all enjoyed.

Left: Ev looking at his geography book.
Right: Frank Capello (Hildegard Kery's son) and Ev.

Fun and Games

When the summer boarders' kids were around we played marbles, jack knife, jacks, pick-up sticks, dominoes, and tiddlywinks. One of the toys I really liked was so simple. It was a piece of round cardboard with two holes in the center and a string going through. You put a loop of string over two fingers and twisted it so when you moved your hands together and apart, the round wheel would whirl around. When the weather was fair we walked in the big fields and woods and the adults would play croquet on the lawn.

Other times, until I went to school, I spent a lot of time alone. We use the word loner but I don't totally buy it – the only time a person is alone is when they sit in a chair and they have no thoughts. You are then alone but you can invite anyone into your company in your thoughts. So though I was often physically solitary, my mind was exceptionally active. My aunt Libbie and others gave me wonderful games and books, such as very small log cabin kit, which allowed me to make a little log cabin with a wood roof like President Lincoln lived in. I also remember building a snowplow at a very young age from a Meccano set and some tin that someone had given me. It was like an erector set with a little battery motor along with all the necessary wheels and gears. You could put most anything together with it. In 1929 when Byrd flew over the South Pole he had a Ford Tri-motor plane. They sold a model airplane kit and my brother Raymond helped me put it together. We also made skis for it and added a string so I could make believe it could land and take off on the snow. Everyone should live in a make-believe land once in their lifetime.

Dunnsville School

Mother finally let me attend school when I was eight, in September 1927, because I could go with Robert and John Stewart, who walked by our house on their way down Settles Hill Road. The one-room schoolhouse was about a mile away, down a steep hill, at the corner of Dunnsville Road (Route 397) and Route 20. The building is now a private house, set back from the road and surrounded by trees. If you drive by there today you can just

Left: Early photo of Dunnsville School.

Right: Ruth Lawyer, Ev's teacher at Dunnsville School.

barely see in the picture windows where the big front door was. With all the brush along the driveway, it's hard to imagine that we used to sleigh ride down to Route 397.

Ruth Lawyer was the one teacher for 13 pupils, who attended up until eighth grade. My grandmother taught there for many years and my mother and her siblings all went there. If you behaved well you could go with a buddy to get water (it took two people to carry the pail) over at Kemner's house well. You'd go past the boy's privy, across the ditch to the well. We all used the same dipper to drink from the pail. So if one person got chicken pox, everybody got chicken pox. One person got measles, everyone got measles. It was very efficient.

I could almost read when I started and by the time I was ten I was able to read the newspaper. Before starting school I had a social studies book. I knew what they made in India and other countries and about the early traders who went to Manchuria. I loved geography. I could draw the coastline of North America from Maine to Virginia when I was eight. I don't think I was overly gifted, but schools back then focused on your strengths, rather than your weaknesses and my circumstances brought out everything that could be brought out of my mind. The exams weren't as difficult as today. People's attitudes were different then. My teacher helped us all to be the best we could be and to believe that we could be smart. If you tell a fish to climb a tree, he'll feel bad all his life. I was never good at English but coming from the farm, I had a knack for mechanical things and good things happened in my life as a result.

That winter, during recess, there was a game (probably fox and geese). I don't remember how the game was played – but I recall that one kid took something from his pocket and laid it by the flagpole. I walked over – thinking nobody saw me – and picked up the brightest dime I had ever seen and put it in my pocket. When recess ended, all nine kids walked in and took our seats and Mrs. Lawyer asked, "Which one of you picked up Robert's dime?" I looked as innocent as I could, but she scanned the nine faces looking back at her and somehow picked out mine. She walked down the aisle and asked me directly, "Do you have the dime?" I had been taught not to lie, so I took it out of my pocket and gave it to her. That simple adventure has stayed with me all these years. I was raised to believe that your family name was your net worth, and at the time I thought that everyone knew about my family situation of poverty and abuse. I was determined to uphold the family name, even at a young age. The very fact that I was caught in the act is the only blemish I've ever caused to the Rau name.

Ev's friends from the Dunnsville School.

Boys in front from left to right: John Stewart, Robert Stewart, Marshall Gray, Ev Rau and Rex (last boy on right unknown).

Funerals

There were three funerals in my eighth year. My older brother Ernest died on June 22, followed by grandfather Peter Ogsbury five days later at the age of 85. Then in November, my father's mother, Augusta Rau died at the age of 86. Of the three deaths, Ernest's hit me the hardest.

Visit to Connecticut.
Top row: Ernest, Uncle Charlie, Aunt Libbie, Raymond.
Bottom row: Ernest's fiancee, Isobel, Mother, Charlie's wife, Everett.

Ernest made friends everywhere and he always had big ideas. I was only three when he asked dad to plow a little hillside because he wanted to go into the horseradish business. When the horseradish didn't work out, Ernest planted a prune orchard with German and Italian plum trees, which was very successful for many years. In fact, I can recall playing in the orchard with the future Altamont florist, Inga Barth, when she and her parents came to pick plums. Next Ernest planted 200 peach trees with visions of reasonable profits. Two years later, when they were blossoming, we had a severe cold spell and all the flower and leaf buds froze. Every one of the trees died, so he hit on another scheme. He rented a piece of property on the corner of Routes 20 and 397, where the auction houses are now. Ernest moved a chicken house down there in the winter on the bobsleigh and opened up an ice cream stand. But for friends and acquaintances (it was Prohibition) he'd lift up a loose floorboard and serve spirits to cheer them up.

In 1924 Ernest went to work as a stock clerk at the W.T. Grant Store in Schenectady. He was promoted quickly and eventually worked in Grant stores in Pennsylvania, Florida, Scranton, Connecticut, and Boston. Each time he got promoted he stopped back at the farm to see the family. When he was named manager of a W.T. Grant Store in Florida, he decided to have surgery to correct a growth in his nose that was affecting his breathing. Soon after the operation, Ernest contracted a sinus infection and came home to recover. But instead the infection got worse. I remember hiding in the closet of the room we shared as he thrashed around and screamed in agony the night he was taken to Ellis hospital. They diagnosed spinal meningitis and put him in an ice bath to bring down his fever. But since it was before antibiotics there was nothing more they could do and he died in terrible pain at the age of 24.

In those days the coffin came to the house for three days before the funeral, and my father, who rarely showed any tenderness, sat with the coffin day and night for three days, quietly singing *"Lay my head beneath the rose where the pinks and violets linger. If I had the wings of an angel o'er these prison walls I would fly. I would fly to the arms of my darling and there I'd be willing to die."* Over the years my father would sing this so often that it became like a soundtrack to my childhood. I don't recall that he ever went back to church after Ernest's funeral.

It seemed like the whole town was at the funeral, but what I remember most clearly was the minister talking about how Ernest would be resurrected in heaven. But as I watched the earth falling on the box during the burial in Fairview Cemetery, I couldn't help imagining how my brother would be trapped in there when he came back to life as the minister had said.

I didn't have long to ponder the question though, because my 85-year-old grandfather died five days later. He was a Civil War veteran who was present at the surrender of Robert E. Lee and was a charter member of the local G.A.R. chapter. Grandfather had been failing over the past year. I recall that most days he sat in a rocking chair in the parlor, not speaking, just twiddling his thumbs, first one way and then the other. In fact I remember that his skin was worn smooth from all the twiddling. One night he fell and hit his head when the hired nurse did not hear him get up to use the commode. He passed away on June 27.

Grandfather's people were among the original families of Guilderland and his life was intertwined with farm and community. He was a staunch Republican and served as town auditor for 22 years. He was a member of St. John's Lutheran church since its

 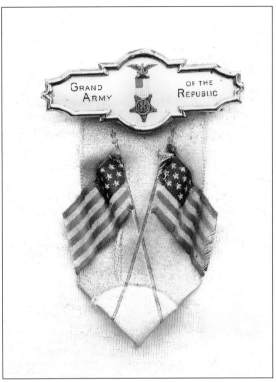

Left: Grandfather Ogsbury in the final year of his life. *Right:* One of Grandfather's prized G.A.R. medals.

founding in 1872 and was an ardent Mason – the last living charter member of the Noah Lodge in Altamont. In his obituary in the *Enterprise*, his brother John D. Ogsbury wrote:

> *A long and useful life has ended; and he has passed on as quietly as he had lived. Scores of friends who knew him will miss the cheery smile, the friendly word of greeting, and the simple hospitality of his home – but these things and many more, will not soon be forgotten.*

Grandfather's funeral, too, was a large affair and left our family exhausted. I didn't realize it at the time, but even at that young age I had absorbed his lessons of living and farming in the old ways and would think of him as a man I could look up to for the rest of my life.

The third funeral was somewhat more distant. We didn't know my father's people well. They lived in Syracuse and travel was expensive in those days. My father's father had died in the 1880s and by the time I came along, his mother was living with her youngest son, Oscar, in their house on Burnet Avenue in Syracuse. She must have been ill for some time because my father and my mother each made trips out to visit during the year.

When we learned of her death in November 1928, Father, Mother, Raymond and I traveled to the funeral in Syracuse. I remember so little of the event. I believe we drove in Raymond's car, and I remember walking down a little alley between two houses because the Raus lived in a flat on the second floor at the back of the large house. I remember Oscar, who I believed worked as a conductor on the railroad, and Charlie who we had seen in Connecticut with Ernest. There was another brother, Max, who had moved to California and eventually lost touch with the family.

Testing Limits

I remember one summer when I was 10 or 12 years old. I'd heard my father talk about going up to the pond. There was a little trail up through the big virgin pines to what we called Lovers Lane. Young people would park near there at night and you'd hear them when they'd get stuck and couldn't get out. Along the way was a section of the woods that the summer boarders referred to as the Cathedral. The hemlocks there were huge, 30" in diameter. There was no vegetation on the ground, just hemlock needles, though at a certain time of year the lady slippers would bloom. On Sundays some of the summer boarders would go up there for religious meditation.

It was a full moonlit night in the middle of summer and I decided to walk through there alone. The countryside was different 80 years ago. There was no chance of bear, no foxes, coyotes, anything like that, because every farm had one or two old family dogs that slept on the back porch during the night. Between the dogs and the fact that there were no hedgerows – no place for animals to hide – the wild animals stayed up north, toward the Adirondacks.

There was very little light available on the forest path. I made my way along by instinct, surrounded by the tall, dark trees. Then, in the darkness I started to notice eyes glowing here and there along the path and off into the woods. I held my breath and waited. As I stood there I recalled what I'd heard about phosphorescent fungi showing light in the darkness after a rain. Though my heart pounded I couldn't quicken my step because I needed to feel my way carefully along the path. From time to time I would startle something, which would hit a little piece of brush and then scatter. And of course the imagination is a powerful mental distractor. Here is a young boy who kowtowed to a very strict father and was working out a way to be himself. When I exited the woods on Settles Hill road that night I was a little different. I stood up a little taller. If I lived another 100 years I would be less afraid because of that night.

Chapter 3

Summer Boarders

I think it was the smiles and friendly conversations of the summer boarders that helped me overcome the silence and sadness of my early days. It was common for farms to offer rooms in summer for extra money and Altamont was developing into a summer destination for Albany and beyond. My father had little appetite for farming and had traveled widely before coming to the farm, so he and my mother decided around 1920 to advertise for boarders in the newspapers. Here's an ad in the *New York Herald* on June 27, 1920.

BOARDERS—A few agreeable people can share the good old farm with us; if you are in need of rest or vigorous recreation can accommodate you with healthful cooking and clean, airy rooms; if beautiful views and large pine forests appeal to you, come spend a few weeks rambling among hills and pines; terms on application. FRANK E. RAU, Altamont, N. Y., R. D. 2.

The boarders came from Brooklyn, Nyack, New Jersey, Yonkers, and Ohio. They would write and ask about availability. The first ones came by train to Altamont and would be picked up at the station in the "surrey with the fringe on top." At the height of the season there would be 22 boarders in nine rooms, paying $14 a week ($22 in later years). Many repeated year after year, because Mother did such an excellent job. Dad remodeled the downstairs to connect the living and dining rooms with a proscenium arch that he designed himself and everyone ate there.

I always laughed that the boarders complained about city smells and then paid to stay on a working farm. But they told me that there was no comparison between the livestock at Pleasant View and the thousands of horses moving through the sweltering streets of New York, Yonkers, or Cleveland. The boarders were an important source of income for our struggling family, but they began tapering off around 1937 or 38 because roadside tourist cabins and restaurants came into being and there were more alternatives for people looking to leave the heat and stench of the city in summer.

Top: Boarders were picked up at the Altamont train station in the "surry with the fringe on top."

Center Left: Mrs. Shannon, Margaret Ruchert, mother, Grandma Ruther, Honey Ruchert, unidentified guest, Sam Shannon, Everett & Old Rex.

Center right: Applicator for bed-bug insecticide.

Below right: Boarders and Ev playing croquet.

As I grew, my first job was to help shoo flies from the dining room. It's a fact that farms have flies and even though we had screen doors, people were going in and out all day and the room would fill up with flies. Just before meals were served, we'd make a lot of noise, wave flags, and the flies would go out in droves. I don't remember that any one ever complained. My other job was to empty the chamber pots once everyone was up and out of their rooms. Each room had a washstand with a large wash bowl and a pitcher of water with a pail to empty the wash water into. I replaced the towels and pails with clean ones. I still remember how proud I was to help the family!

Electricity came in 1938 but the farm didn't have indoor plumbing until 1949. Though Mother had two hired girls to help, it's hard to imagine how she managed to cook and clean for so many people without plumbing. On Monday she turned the rooms over to get ready for the next round of boarders. There was a big horse chestnut tree near the side of the house with a wooden washing machine underneath in the shade. It had a lever, like a rack and pinion and beaters that reminded me of a milking stool. I spent hours washing clothes every Monday, unless it was raining. It took two people to snap the sheets taut before hanging on the clothesline to minimize wrinkles, and then two people to fold them. Besides the laundry, Mother took each bed totally apart once a boarder left and dusted for bedbugs. She used a little duster, shaped like an upside down oil can that she unscrewed and put powder in. She used to squirt this bug-killing powder under each bed slat. Having linoleum on the floors instead of carpets was also a big help. It must have worked because there never were complaints from the guests.

We loved it when boarders came because Dad would behave so well. The boarders enjoyed talking to the gentlemanly farmer-proprieter, and a few even helped with some of the farm work. Many came back year after year and became like family with hugs all around when they arrived and when they left. I wasn't really aware of class back then, but when I think about it now, the boarders must have been fairly well off. As time went on, they came in big cars, outfitted for traveling. Everyone dressed up on Sundays. Tie, collars, everything. Some of them would go to church, but others would picnic up in the woods in a clearing of old growth pines they called *the Cathedral*. Though some would travel about and go sightseeing, many spent their days in rocking chairs on the front porch, watching the neighborhood.

Most stayed a week or two but there were a few, like the Shannons from Ohio, who stayed the season. Sam was a salesman, whose route included upstate New York. His wife made beautiful paper flowers for sale. She would bring all her materials and sit on the porch making artificial flowers, which she would sell when she returned home. Mr. Winterbottom was a New York City undertaker. He drove up in his Packard touring car with the expandable racks along the running board, which always made me think of gypsies. His son, Harry, was my age (I was 8 then). When they went home, they took me back with them and I stayed at their estate in Nyack. While I was visiting they took me into New York to the Chrysler Building. The upper windows did not have glass at that time. I was so enthralled while looking out that I leaned out farther than was safe and someone took me by the shoulder and pulled me back. It might have been my last trip to New York!

Jim Sheridan was a Willard Battery salesman who later became a GM executive. He and his wife Rita would stay for quite awhile in the summer. One year they took me down to see the Ziegfeld Follies in New York City and this farm boy became aware of his "natural health" watching the Rockette dancers! That natural health would be tested by another boarder some years later. I don't remember her name, but she was single, quite loud, and about 40 years old. I was 15 or 16 at the time. She noticed me outside doing chores and started chatting. She pointed to the big field that had scattered pine trees and asked if I would go with her where she would show me a good place to enjoy nature. Even in my innocence, I knew she wasn't interested in nature, so I told her I was busy.

The last boarders I remember were "Uncle John" Henger and his blind sister. She would walk through this house without help because she knew the steps. It was as if, in her mind, she could see as well as you or I. She sat knitting with everyone else on the front porch and when dinner was served she would walk in and sit down. She would drink her coffee and always set the cup down in the same place. Her brother would tell her where her food was on her plate (12:00, 8:00, etc.). She ate neatly. Never spilled. They came for many years and became a part of the family. When John left the last time in 1937 or 38, he came in to say goodbye to me and my mother. For the first time, I felt like I could see the love emotion. So pure. So white. Though he didn't kiss my mother when he said good bye, he laid his hand on her arm. "Well. I won't be coming back. I have to say goodbye." This connection must have been like a gift to my mother in the midst of all her anxiety and sadness. I never will forget it.

Left: John Henger often helped with farm chores. Here he is sitting on the hay rake. *Right*: Thacher Park was a popular destination for boarders. Father holds onto his hat as the Ruchert family from Albany pose near the Indian Ladder Trail.

Chapter 4

Farming

Most people work to make a living, but with farming you make a life. And though I've worked on and off the farm throughout my life, I have always been a farmer. I've had the unique experience of learning to farm from men who walked behind horse-drawn plows and I've seen the many benefits (and broken promises) of later scientific farming. Our farm has always raised both animals and crops, for sale and for our family. We used early fruit tree spray sparingly and never got into GMO crops. Today my son and grandson are learning how to renew the farm using organic methods that are easily grafted onto the honest heritage of an earlier time.

I must have been five or six when I watched my father plow a small field for Ernest's horseradish project. I can see Dad driving the team of horses and using what, in my childhood mind seemed like excessive force. Now that I'm older, I recognize that he didn't give the proper commands, so the horses didn't know what he wanted them to do. He got so frustrated trying to get the plowing done that he yanked the reigns really hard. Not growing up on a farm, he hadn't yet learned that working with animals required cooperation rather than coercion. When Uncle Willard or Grandfather plowed, it took the slightest pull on the reins, because they worked the horses all the time.

The era of horse farming ended around 1930 when our remaining horse, Star, had to be put down. My father said that her teeth were too far gone and she would not survive another winter. We walked her down to the Pasture lot, where my father put her humanely to sleep. I hadn't given much thought to the horse in years until one day our boys came running in to ask about the big bones they'd discovered down in the old Pasture lot.

By 1929 the country was sliding into the Depression. What happened to our economy in 2008 was pale by comparison to what happened in the Great Depression. And what you read in the history books is only a shadow of the psychological and emotional trauma that people went through. We saw pictures in the *Knickerbocker News* of bread lines in the cities and were thankful that we still had summer boarders, that we were still selling eggs in Schenectady, and that there was always food on the table. But the debts

Top: Grandfather showing Ev how to use a spring tooth harrow.

Middle left: Father with piglets.

Middle right: Ray and Ev picking chickens

Lower right: Father and Ev collecting a swarm of bees.

Facing Page
Left: Father and brother Raymond harvesting oats on an 1898 reaper and binder and Raymond's 1929 Farmall Tractor. Ev sitting on an axle holding on. Uncle Willard and hired man are in the field. About 1930.

Right: Charlie Lainhart with a load of loose hay on an F-12 tractor around 1935.

were piling up and our family was wrestling with its own kind of depression. The funerals the year before and my father's antagonism to farming was taking its toll on the farm.

My brother Raymond was 23 and I was 10. He was living at home and helping on the farm while he commuted in the Model T to his job at General Electric in Schenectady. There he worked on the line, making monitor top refrigerators. In 1929 the line was shut down and he lost his job. Though a hard blow for Raymond, this was the best thing that could have happened to Pleasant View Farm. At the time the farm was being focused on broiler hens and eggs for sale, along with food for the family. From the outside you might notice that the German threshing barn, which had been built for cows sometime before 1800, was leaning slightly. Inside, however, you'd see that its roof was so bad that Dad had jerry rigged a second roof inside, by taking 2x4s and adding roof boards and tar paper. Unfortunately, the other barn wasn't set up for cows, so Dad had been selling them off a little at a time so he could invest in chickens, which were in good demand.

Raymond had energy and new ideas. He sized up the potential: 60 acres of open land – weedy with two-to-four inch white pine trees, growing up 10-15 feet high. There were some hills with thin soil and some flat land with good ground that had eroded off the hills. Thankfully Ray decided to invest his time and money into turning the farm around, starting with buckwheat. He was impressed by what he saw in Mr. Fick's new tractor dealership and bought the first Farmall Regular tractor in the area. It had a two-bottom plow, disk harrow, spring tooth harrow, heavy duty hay wagon, hay rake, and a reaper and binder. Though not robust, I helped out as much as I could when the fields needed to be cleared of trees. My job was to hook a chain high up on a sapling so Raymond could pull it with the tractor. Once the sapling came down a bit it was rehooked and pulled out.

In the days of the horse plow, you would plow about six inches deep. The tractor plowed eight inches, so we were bringing up new and bigger stones, which had to be picked off. I wasn't strong enough to plow but I needed to be there because the plow had

a spring hitch and when it met an immovable stone it would automatically unhitch. When it unhitched, Ray backed up the tractor, positioned it and I had to raise up the hitch and drop it in the clevis to continue plowing again. We picked the stones off of 60 acres before planting the seed so they wouldn't damage the machines when we planted or harvested the grain. Once we started plowing I walked behind the plow on every inch of this farm. I rose to the occasion because here was an important job for me to do to help my family.

That of course is one of the most exciting times of my life. I don't know how many thousands of miles I walked behind that plow. I walked behind it for years. I loved seeing the weeds turn over and disappear. After clearing and plowing the land that year, we sowed buckwheat around the fourth of July so it would blossom after the 95 degree days in August. (Heat blights the blossoms and decreases the yield.) Buckwheat grows 18 to 36 inches tall with many coin shaped leaves that totally shade the ground and limit weeds, which makes it easy to grow. We harvested the buckwheat in September with a reaper and binder. We created shocks that were set up in groups of five with four in a square and one spread out on top like a cap. In the event of rain, this would keep the grain dry and even allow it to dry quickly.

Once the buckwheat was dry in the field, we'd call Earl Gray, the thresher man. Back then, you were dependent on the guy who owned the threshing machine. He made appointments with all the farmers. If there was a delay – like bad weather – they would thresh in order, even if it meant that your grain got wet. It was axiomatic to respect the authority of the thresher. I can't recall any animosity among neighbors over threshing or other communal chores. It was about survival. To survive as a farmer you needed to be neighborly with two or three other people and all work together.

We sold the buckwheat to Parkis Mills in Galway. They were producing a popular product called *Jolly Farmer Pancake Mix*, an early packaged food. There was big demand and their trucks took the mix to the major cities. Mother was even able to buy it in the general store in Altamont. After a few years growing buckwheat we switched to corn, oats and wheat. The fields were almost weedless now because the buckwheat shaded out the weeds. It was our nontoxic weed killer. Today if you take care of the land as we did years ago and are willing to learn to read the soil you can farm successfully without the use of toxic sprays. I have lived 95 years without them.

Threshing

Threshing day in the 1930s was the most exciting time of the year. The reward of storing God's bounty in the grainery was enjoyed like a lucky lottery ticket in today's world. For me as a kid it was a friendly romantic workday because the neighbors came. One of my jobs was to have a tub of water ready for dinner at noon. There was a long low bench made with a plank with four legs in it. There would be a porcelain washtub and several big towels. I put cold spring water there in the morning. By noontime there'd be a little bit of heat from the summer sun to warm the water. At noontime dinner all the men would come up to wash and they were always friendly to the younger kids. There would be huge platters of beef stew with potatoes, carrots and whatever was in season in the garden, all heavy with good-seasoned, salted gravy. Everyone would take a slice of bread and butter and use it to wipe their plates because the gravy tasted so good. It was the romance of my life, to see our friendly loving helpful neighbors eating in our home. I never saw any discord. If so, they hid it because there was a job to do – for us and for their own threshing needs. It was cooperative. Everybody helped everyone and nobody kept score. Kids worked as go-fers. "Get a pail of water with a metal dipper!" How pleasant to taste that cold spring water on a hot summer day.

In 1932 we put in hay with the Lainharts. Neither farm could do it alone. My second cousin, Reid Lainhart, and I loaded the wagons with the hay loader. I was the back man. I loaded the back half and passed half the hay to the front to Reid. The hay loader went over the wind rows and picked up the hay and dropped it all up in the back of the wagon. I had to take forkfuls and deposit them next to each other across the wagon, because that's how you tied a load of hay together. Do that the same up to the middle of the wagon. Half had to be pitched to the front of the wagon for Reid to do the same thing. It was called binding the load and though it was hard work, we were happy to know that we were supporting the family with a crop that was so important for the horses, cows, sheep, and for sale. We had four barns to fill. The Lainharts have a Dutch barn and a horse barn and our Dutch barn and big hay barn had a loft. In old barns, where there are big timbers, you'll find round poles 2-3 inches apart. You'd put the hay carefully up there on those poles so it could dry out and breathe. We filled the barns right up to the peak. As you got near the peak you had to work bent over because the roofing nails would scratch your back if you weren't careful.

It took about seven weeks to do the hay and to fill up these four barns, with many visits to the Bozenkill for skinny dipping to cool off on hot nights. During June and July, Venus looks like a bright star after the sun has gone down. One crystal-clear night during haying – we worked until dark – I remember looking up at that shining star. "Star light star bright, first star I see tonight. I wish I may I wish I might have the wish I wish tonight!" My wish was to find a girl who could be the mother of my children and I could finish my life with her. Somehow or other that worked out pretty well.

The grain combine came to our farm about 1938 and this was the beginning of the end of neighbor helping neighbor on the farm. Now young men and girls could work at jobs off the farm. We paid a farmer to combine our grain. We didn't need a work crew anymore. In fact, by 1939 old-world farming was almost all over with in Dunnsville. The Lainharts had a few cows but had pretty much gone out of the farming business. My brother went back to work for G.E. and I found work there myself in 1939. It was a big change that took the romance out of my everyday life.

Corn

Dad and I cut field corn below the house, making corn shocks as we went, using a "corn horse." We took a piece of wood, like a 2x4, with two holes drilled through one end. Poles were placed in these holes, which became legs. This end of the corn horse was about 30 inches off the ground. The other end rested on the ground. Midway was a horizontal third hole which contained a broomstick. We would walk down the row cutting corn with a corn knife until we each had an armload of corn stalks. We'd set bundles of corn around the broomstick until the corn shock was about five feet in diameter at the bottom or big enough to stand the wind. We tied it with foxtail grass. You twist the grass together the way the reapers tied their grain bundles before twine was invented. You can see hand tying demonstrations at the Altamont Fair. Once the corn shock was tied, we would pull the broomstick out of the top, and slide the corn horse out from the side and go on to the next location. The corn shocks stood that way until they were brought up to the barn.

Back then we had a lot of pheasants in the fields because they had plenty of corn to eat. If they picked one kernel out of a cob, some others would drop in the ground. Add the brushy fruits growing in the hedgerows and the pheasants could survive all winter.

Before the first heavy snow you set several posts outside the barn and put boards across the top. You'd lean those bundles of corn so their tops were close together, which would shed most of the water if it rained or snowed. Later, after fall plowing was finished you would have a husking bee. Twenty or thirty people would crowd inside the barn with lanterns all around. You'd bring the shock into the barn and lay it on the floor. Three or four strong guys would pick the corn off with the husks on and throw them to the people sitting around. To husk the corn, you use a little tool – a piece of leather hooked over your finger with a sharp wooden peg. That point loosened the dry husks off the corn ears so you could pull the husks down. If you didn't use the tool your fingers would wear out because the corn husks are hard and dry and sharp. If you got the occasional red ear you could walk around the circle and kiss whoever you'd like – much to the dismay of some young women and the joy of older men.

Chickens

Though the buckwheat was successful and easy to grow, in 1936 we switched to corn, wheat, and oats for our 300 laying hens, which had been carefully raised from small chicks purchased from the Zimmerman chicken hatchery in Gallupville in early spring. We bought mash from the mill in Guilderland Center, next to the railroad tracks and grew our own scratch feed, but we could also feed them wheat and oats. In the 1930 census. Father and Raymond each listed their profession as "chicken farmer," which provided a steady income supplemented by the successful buckwheat crops and summer boarders.

Before then, we had always had chickens, but it seemed like everyone else did too. Before 1900 most folks lived on farms and raised their own food. Those days chickens were not confined. You hunted the eggs all over, without knowing when they'd been laid. I remember collecting eggs when I was small, though the egg basket is quite large and it's most likely that I picked up the eggs and gave them to someone else who was carrying the basket. If you had a few surplus eggs, you sold them. When cooking, you didn't break an egg into a bowl with the flour. You broke it into a little dish to see if it was fresh. If there was an odor, you threw it to a dog.

As cities grew, there weren't enough farmers with outdoor flocks of chickens to supply the demand, so the cooperative extension began looking for ways to help farmers increase production. In order for chickens to lay an egg a day when you keep them confined, they've got to drink quite a bit of water. As a result, their droppings are very moist, which means you have to work to keep the litter dry or the chickens will get sick. The most challenging time in a chicken house, therefore, is a warm spell after freezing winter weather when the droppings thaw and the litter gets wet.

By 1930 we had seven coops for 300 chickens, which was a total of 1,008 square feet or about three square feet per bird. Chickens do most of their pooping at night, while

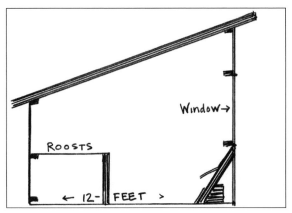

Farmer science:
The 12x12 Cornell chicken coop consisted of a lean-to with a door on one side. There was a 6-8 foot hinged panel that you could open for ventilation — even during inclement weather. The big door on the front of the building faced south, so it could be open for air to let sunshine in. If humidity was down, this would dry the litter.

Ev and Raymond surrounded by the chicken flock about 1929.

they're roosting, so the back of coop had a solid wood shelf raised above the floor, and they would roost above that. The roof was only a couple of feet above the roost, which cut down on drafts and air movement. During the winter it would stay warm enough to keep the chickens from freezing as poultry has a higher body temperature than humans. And there was enough room down below the roost to get a wheelbarrow in to clean out the poop.

I'll never forget, one day when I was young, my dad took an egg from one of the hatchling chicks after about four days under a setting hen and broke it for me. On the yolk was a little red dot with tiny red lines radiating out. He told me that the heart formed first and that this was the beginning of the chicken. They're different from other animals or humans. Once fertilized, the protein in the white of the egg realigns and attaches all of the necessary proteins to make the baby chick. Meanwhile the yolk stays intact and is absorbed by the chick after it's hatched, before it can eat and drink on its own.

Chicks or turkey poults are shipped through the mail. If they're hatched Sunday and mailed Monday, they arrive Wednesday. One time I received a delivery of turkeys that didn't feel right. I figured that somewhere along the line they'd been kept in a place that was too warm, because when I lifted the box they were light. I opened the box and dipped each turkey's head in water and then dipped it in the mash. I did this twice and when I checked the coop during the day I found three or four lying prostrate. I made sure to dip their beaks in the water again. We only lost two out of fifty turkeys. "The eye of the master fattens the calf."

There's one disease they call coccidiosis that will kill chickens in the first couple of weeks if your coop isn't clean and dry. My parents would dissolve lye and use it to clean the coops. It worked, except one really wet May during the Depression. I remember watching my father go into the chicken house with a wheelbarrow and coming out with it partially full of dead baby chicks. We had to mortgage the farm to recover from that disastrous season. I've seen videos of modern farmers going down the line with an inoculation hose full of antibiotics. I can't believe what we're eating in our meat.

Picking Chickens

To cut down on contamination and flies before refrigeration, the early farmers would sell chickens, turkey and geese that were picked but not gutted. All poultry was picked dry and the people who got used to doing it could go really fast. Today you kill the bird and when it is motionless you plunge it into hot water. You yank the bird up and down in the water and the water goes farther into the feather follicles. Once a wing feather comes out it's ready and you can start picking the feathers. I guess the water has to have cooked the skin partially to release the grip that it had on the feathers.

Pigs

My uncle Willard Ogsbury came back to the farm to live when I was 15 and still in high school. This is when I got the first taste of real farming. We always had pigs, but when Willard came, we saved sows and bred them and they had 77 piglets, which he helped me raise through the summer. The farm grainery was full that year. We had a 40-gallon cooker with a firebox under it. Willard would fill the cooker with grain and water and simmer or slow cook it all day. This saved grinding fees. We did buy 55 gallon barrels of feed that looked like yogurt, and we bought an electric fence charger. The pigs had four acres of lush pasture to run and they grew very nicely. I sold them for seven cents a pound dressed weight, which netted $1075. It was a mortgage lifter and was the first time I had my own money to spend.

Butchering

In today's world few farmers butcher their own hogs, but when I was young it was a well-orchestrated, highly skilled craft in which everyone involved knew their role and worked smoothly together. Skilled workers managed to catch, hold and process a 350 pound pig safely and quickly.

As a kid, I loved the spirit of camaraderie and learned to do two jobs. The first was sharpening a knife so you could shave a pig with it. The second was cleaning the small intestines for sausage casings. An intestine is made up of three layers. There's an outer layer of soft protein, a hard layer of tissue, which is the casing, and an inner layer of soft protein. There was always a little piece of green brush someplace. You cut it off and split it so there is a sharp V at the end. You dragged the 24-inch long intestine through the V to clean the outer surface – both ways until it was really clean. My father carved a special stick about

24 inches long with a tiny little angled groove on the top. I put the end of the intestine on the end of the stick and rolled the intestine over to turn it inside out. Now the soft protein would be on the outside and I could clean it in the "V" just as I did the outside. When they were totally clean (and boy they better be clean) I would submit the casings for inspection, "That isn't clean, do it right!" Once I was finished, I washed the casing with water and vinegar. The next step was to layer the clean casings into a little crock that was prepared with a half inch of salt in the bottom: layer of salt, layer of casings, etc. They dry hard. When we were ready to make sausage, we would soak the casings in lukewarm water. They stretch and are very strong and flexible. I always liked to slide the casing onto the horn of the sausage stuffer and make links by twisting the casing with just one revolution.

This was a great time in my life. There was always so much friendly joking and laughter. People worked hard but had fun doing it. Then of course we did butchering on three farms in all. My children, Ken and Tim especially, and Ernie, would like nothing better than to do that once more, and they just might yet, because we have all the tools.

Root Cellar

One of the earliest jobs I can remember was sorting apples in the spring. My parents would open the outside cellar door and take a barrel of apples and lean it over sidewise on the steps so I could lean in and reach the apples. The Ben Davis apple is an excellent keeper. Come the end of February, middle of March, some of them would be rotten, but the good ones would be okay. It's not the best tasting apple in the world but if that's the only fruit you had, it was the best. That orchard was probably planted after the Civil War by Peter Ogsbury and has been there as long as I can remember. We still have one of the original old apple trees. This year I hope to take a scion and graft it onto another tree so we can keep it into the future.

In my childhood, the unheated cellar had a dirt floor and very little heat at night in the winter. The dirt floor was a wonderful place to store cabbage. You keep growing cabbage in the ground until it gets really cold. If you know you're going to get a lot of rain, you go out and take the cabbage head firmly and twist it a little over half a turn to shear some of the roots off. Then it'll slowly grow through the rainy fall without splitting. Most people pick cabbage early now, but you don't have to. It can tolerate a light frost. You don't want to put it down in the cellar when the cellar is too warm, so you leave it in the ground till the last possible day. Then you pull the whole cabbage up and put it upside down on the damp cool floor and it's good till February. You leave the roots sticking up in the air. And of course when you cut them off, they go to the pigs or chickens. We made a lot of sauerkraut with that cabbage. It was a good vegetable to spice up a soup or five o'clock meal.

Controlling Rats and Mice

My mother would put about six inches of water in the bottom of a 10-gallon crock. Then she'd take a piece of heavy brown paper, cut a cross in the center and smear bacon fat in the center of the paper. The paper would go over the crock and be secured with strong string. She'd prop a slanting board up from the floor to the top edge of the crock. Rats would smell the bacon grease, walk up the board, and slide down into the crock where they were trapped and drowned.

When you have a lot of grain you're bound to have mice, which is why we always had a bunch of cats. They liked to hang around because at milking time we had a wooden carved trough we'd put milk in. One cat could drink out of the stream while milking. Owls were another way to control pests naturally. In the upper part of a Dutch barn there are generally two holes in the gable end so you can see to get hay in the daytime. They were called martin or owl holes, because the tiny barn owls would go in there. With their uncanny sight and hearing they would make quick work of any mouse that dared to go up on top the hay.

Pigeons

Barns are rough finished on the inside, and when they're sided there's a one-inch edge from the overlap of the siding on the inside of the barn. Holding onto the studs or the back of the siding and resting my feet on the top edge of the siding, I could climb the inside of the barn like a ladder. There were pigeon nests up on high ledges near the roof. At the right time of year, mother would send me up there for squabs. I'd put them in my pocket and climb down. Very few people have eaten squab pie, but I have. For some it's a delicacy. For us it was survival!

Milk

Our milk, before refrigeration, was put on what my mother called a swing. The cellar had big beams and they had nailed some vertical pieces to the beams and added cross pieces to make a little deck. They put tin up there so any mouse that could climb across the side of the timber would hit the tin and fall back down. That's where the milk pans sat. The next day you'd take a skimmer with small holes in the center, skim under the cream and dump it into a bucket. Mother either made fresh cream butter or let it sour and churned it to make sour cream butter and delicious buttermilk. Milk doesn't sour in 24 hours. Maybe 36 but not before if kept at a certain temperature. For years I had the dipper my uncle used when he delivered raw milk in Altamont. A person would come out of the house to his wagon with their bucket. He submerged the dipper into the milk can. He did that every day. Rain or shine.

The best cheese I ever ate was made from cottage cheese. Mother hung the cottage cheese in a bag to let the whey drip out and then added a little butter so it would form a ball. She put the ball on a saucer with a deep soup bowl over the top and left it on the stone cellar steps for two weeks. When you took the cover off you would see a fine mold — long fibers with little balls on the end. Once you scraped that off, the cheese was so delicious! I can't forget the taste. You have to have the right place to cure it. You need 45 or 50° with high humidity to grow the mold. I think the refrigerator would be too cold.

How to Make a Mulberry Pie

When the berries are ripe, sew clean old bedsheets together and get the kids to hold them up under the mulberry tree. Send Father out onto the thick branches as far as he can go and have him shake the tree until the berries fall. Collect the berries, pick out the leaves and twigs. Mix three cups of berries with one cup of sugar and some flour and fill a pie crust. Cover the top with more crust and bake in a 350° oven for 45 minutes.

Firewood

We worked with Millard Gray to cut our firewood using an early hit and miss engine to power one of the first circular buzz saws. I was too young to be outside because it was very dangerous. When I was finally big enough to watch, I had to obey and stay over there!! So you don't get hurt. Millard Gray was the father of Earl Gray, the threshing machine man. I have great respect for them. They were cutting wood to keep the house warm. The average fireplace uses 15 cord of wood in a season. Since our black iron cook stove used less wood and gave more steady heat, the kitchen was the warmest room in the house.

You had to be sure to use dry seasoned wood in the wood cook stove. Otherwise you risked chimney fire. We had one once when I was a boy. Raymond and my father soaked a rug in a washtub and carried it up to the roof and laid it over the top of the chimney and smothered the flames. Eventually the fire went out without causing major damage. We were lucky. Or my folks were mentally trained by the close exchange of ideas and experiences with our neighbors.

Dangers

Farms can be dangerous places. You can ask my kids how many million times I told them not to do this or that because you might get hurt. The instinct was so ingrained, like sadness. It came from stories I heard as a boy from my uncle Willard, like the man who was raking hay, who raked a bee's nest. The bees got after the horses and he fell off the hay rake — not backwards but forwards — and he rolled over and over until he died. There is another story that has always stood out in my mind. One day a local family was cutting hay and a young boy was in the field. Somehow, tragically, they cut his legs off at the ankles.

Grandfather, the hired man, and Uncle Willard using an early hit and miss engine to cut firewood. Millard Gray is at the far end. Father is taking photo. 1926.

Enough of those things happened that, though it didn't set fear in my mind, it really sharpened it.

By sharing intelligence we knew, for example, that when chopping wood with an ax you always have your legs far apart because if the ax happened to bounce off the mark it could hit your foot. Everybody kept their ax razor sharp because the sharp ax cut better and was not as likely to bounce off and hit your foot. Thankfully we become the type of person we are, by the people we've associated with. My parents, grandparents, uncles and aunts all carried on with basic safety precautions. At an early age my mind heard these lessons, and with the help of the lord we had few serious injuries and the ones we had have all healed.

Roads in the winter snow

When I was a boy, it was each farmer's responsibility to keep their wagon lanes open between their property lines. A farmer typically had a huge wooden roller that he pulled with teams of horses. The rollers were six feet in diameter and 8-10 feet long. They were divided into two sections so they would turn easier. The snow was rolled down and then

Earl Gray standing with his wife Viola Gray, Shirley Anthony, and Billy Kemner in the 1940s.

further compacted by the horse's hooves. When blizzards came through, if the road was on the east side of the hill the fair-weather west wind that followed the blizzard would drift snow two to three feet high or more. If the snow was in an area where it drifted higher, the doctors and the mailmen had the authority to snip the barbed wire fence wires and go around the drifts through the fields to call on patients or deliver mail.

A farmer would also take a big freight bobsleigh and go back and forth to make a track. If there was a winter thaw and he was expecting rain that would freeze, my father chained the land plow to the rear of the bobsleigh and widened the rut where the sleigh went. This way, if it rained and then went to zero they would have made the track a little wider so it wasn't hard ice that the bobsleigh had to go through.

A lingering winter memory of childhood is our neighbor Leslie Stewart and family turning onto Lainhart road from Settles Hill Road on Sunday morning. He had chime bells that were attached to the pole between the team of horses and also smaller round bells on the strap that went around the horse's belly. When Leslie turned the corner he would slow down and then speed the horses up to a jog. This would ring the chimes and the little bells, making a very pleasant sound. To this day I can hear Leslie Stewart going by on his way to the Reformed Church in Altamont. Though I was a poor country boy, we were rich in happiness, spirit, and hope for better times.

Seasons

I've always respected and loved the four seasons on the farm. In spring the whole world is a lawn. The grass grows, the crops grow. Fall was romantic because it's harvest time and that's what kept the animals and family nourished with some money besides. Winter is beautiful. When the moon shines on a fresh fall of snow you can see little diamond flakes. And if you happen to get a sleet storm on top of snow you can see the reflection of the moon across the sloping fields right to where you're standing. I still love listening to falling and drifting snow. This farm is situated such that if you have a fresh fall of snow it's usually followed by a cold front with very little wind but every once in awhile you have snow devils – little snow tornadoes. In spring I used to walk down through the ravines where there would be ice and water running underneath that made a trickling sound. My little serenade. And as farmers, we always like the rain, even though a thundershower might wash out the fields. Though I have always respected the dangers of a heavy storm with lightning and the immediate crash of thunder, I also remember somewhere in the bible it says "Be still and know that I am God."

Upper left: Ev walking to meet Kelly de la Rocha for a *Schenectady Gazette* interview in 2014. Photo by Patrick Dodson.
Upper right: View from the house to the east in early summer 2013.
Lower left: View from the terrace to the east in late fall 2007.
Lower right: View to the east after an ice storm.

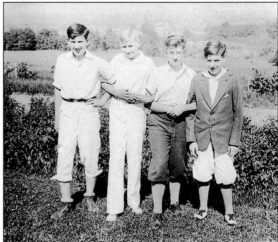

Top left: Scoutmaster Bill Clark and Ev.
Middle left: From the Boyscout Jamboree souvenir pennant.
Lower left: Log cabin built by Ev and Joe Soraghan.
Upper right: Ev with Mother ready for the Boyscout Jamboree in 1937.
Lower right: Joe Soraghan (left), Ev and two other boys.

Chapter 5

Growing Taller

Though we never went hungry during the Depression, we never had a lot of extra money, which became an issue when I entered high school. Though still shy, I had done well at the one-room Dunnsville school and felt pretty much at home with everyone there. But being a farm kid in high school was another story. Besides the shame I felt toward my father's misbehavior, it was hard to adjust to the larger high school. Everett Ross, Kirby Van Zandt, Bob Ritchie, Dave Cowan, Keith Fryer, Wayne Gaige, and Mathew Hofnagel soon became good friends. My farm friends and I were often taunted by the village kids. They said we had the smell of cows on us. And we did! We did chores before school and didn't change our clothes. We didn't have time for that. I walked two miles each way to school – or skied when drifts closed the roads – and my good friend Dave Cowan, who lived just below old Knowersville on a dairy farm, walked to school also. (His stable wasn't ventilated and I have to say he actually did have a very good farm odor sometimes!) When we got back to school after Thanksgiving my freshman year, my so-called good friends were comparing the size of their turkey dinners and turned to me and asked, "What did *you* have for Thanksgiving, *Rau*?" Of course they knew we couldn't afford a turkey, but the way they said my name made me stand tall and say, proudly, that we'd had a very delicious rooster along with other tasty dishes. And mom's pie was the best.

From that time on I was determined to show the world that the Rau name was a good name. Somewhere along the way God gave me the ability to see that I was not associated with the bad decisions of others – except through memory. I looked for every opportunity to show what I could do. I had always been involved in 4-H and Boy Scouts and I competed whenever possible and volunteered for leadership roles. I was thrilled when my friend Dave Cowan's father, who was the rural mailman, gave me a quarter one winter day to deliver the mail up Settles Hill Road to a corner with five mail boxes. The road was absolutely impassible. I walked up and down huge drifts. I didn't do it for the money. It was important to me to be trusted – to be recognized to carry the U.S. Mail. That trust was better than my pay, though the quarter was nice too. I probably gave it to my mother to put in the coffee can for home expenses.

Beyond school activities I also found other ways to distinguish myself. In winter I used to ski down Lainhart Road and into Altamont for school. Skis back then were different than they are today, with their quick-release bindings. These were wooden skis with metal bindings that hooked onto your boots and God forbid you would fall. One day in my second year I bet my friends that I could climb up to High Point, where the talus slope meets the Helderberg escarpment just above Altamont, during lunch and ski back in time for afternoon classes. I had hiked up there many times with the Boy Scouts, and I was in pretty good shape. I put my skis and poles across my shoulders and headed up the trail. The snow was too deep to walk so I had to herringbone (point the skis out for steep climbing). About halfway up I came across a large tree that had fallen across the trail. Luckily the snow pack was pretty deep and I marked the spot in memory so I would stop there on the way down. Once I reached the top I called to my friends. The air was clear and cold and I could hear them answer, "Good Fun!" On the way down I was able to use a jerked Christy – a quick 90 degree turn – to stop so I could side step over the fallen tree and finish skiing down. It took about thirty minutes to climb up to the top of the talus slope and about 5 minutes to ski down to the village. Flying down into the school yard, I think everyone was out there to see whether I would make it. After that, I didn't have so many issues with respect.

My high school career (along with everything else) almost ended during my freshman year. I had walked down to Altamont with my mother and father for a Christmas party at Irving Lainhart's. As soon as I got there I started feeling awful. I stayed at the party a little while, but when I had a terrible splitting headache and was sick to my stomach we decided to walk back up the hill. By the time we arrived home I had a raging fever and Mother put me to bed. Dr. Cullen came in the morning and diagnosed scarlet fever. He reached into his bag full of little corked test tubes and gave us various medicines. I was confined to bed for several weeks and was still too weak to be outside until the dandelions were blooming. By then I could also keep down a bowl of thick tomato soup – and it tasted so good! Unfortunately, because I had missed so much school they made me repeat the grade, so it took me five years to graduate.

I didn't really have friends to run around with until the last couple of years of high school. You can't call it running around, because that's what people do today. I went to birthday parties attended by six to twenty kids, though I felt too self conscious to dance. There were other parties, such as the Valentines Day party we attended in the big white house on the corner of Main and Euclid Ave. owned by Mr. and Mrs. Kent, the history and mathematics teachers. Reid Lainhart and I rode down in his dad's old car. We got down where Route 397 is now and crossed the bridge. The hill was snowed in and we had to shovel our way up the hill. When we finally finished, we went to the party. When we arrived there must have been 25 kids playing spin the bottle. Back then we didn't kiss the way you see on TV today. There was just a touch of the lips and that was that. If the bottle stopped at a girl who normally wasn't overly friendly, you faced a mental situation – is she going to let me kiss her or not?

My neighbor Joe Soraghan was my age and we did many good things together through the years, including fishing and hunting. We trapped too, and sold the furs. But the best thing was building a small log cabin in the woods to play President Lincoln. The cabin was about 8 by 9 feet and made of clear straight pine trees we scavenged in the woods after a fire. We even created door jams and gable ends and a tar paper roof. Many years later, when it was damaged in a storm, we rebuilt it in the orchard in sight of the house for our kids to play in.

Mother was not big on college, but my neighbor Joe's mother convinced me I should study Latin. I do remember *puella, puer, agricola* and that's it. However, she did have an influence in other ways. She was involved with the State Theater in Schenectady, where they had stage shows. She coached the drama class in Altamont High School and she got me involved. Here I was, a poor farmer, and when they did *A Christmas Carol* by Dickens, I was Bob Cratchett, the one who carried the crippled Tiny Tim. My father made the sets by painting two screens in the Masonic Temple's stage to give the illusion of depth. Hearing applause from so many friends in the huge Masonic Temple on Maple Avenue in Altamont was something that made me grow a little taller.

After that we staged *Old Louisiana,* a love story. I was the LEAD. I can't tell you how petrified I was to kiss a girl. I had never kissed a girl in public. I had never even hugged a girl. In rehearsal I didn't kiss the girl but during the performance I did, though I didn't enjoy it since we had over 100 friends there who were ready to make fun of me.

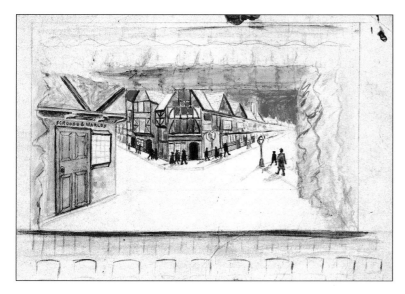

This is a watercolor sketch Ev's father made for the scenic back-drop for *A Christmas Carol,* which he painted. It filled the back of the Masonic Lodge.

After the play, I was invited to the leading lady's home for dinner. I suppose her parents wanted to see who I was and how I acted out in public. I was embarrassed to go because I didn't have the right clothes. All my clothes were hand downs and many were patched. They were very nice but it wasn't a comfortable dinner for me and I never spoke to her again.

Academics

As a young child I received a practical education on the farm and a very positive approach to learning at the Dunnsville School. I think that's why, through my life, even if I couldn't understand the modern things, I never felt dumb. In high school I would tackle anything, not knowing if I'd succeed. If I succeeded I felt good and if the problem was beyond my reason to solve, based on the information I already had stored in my brain – I never felt dumb or had to resort to any exotic action to prove myself. The most important thing I learned was that if you can't accomplish one project, you have to go back and review the successful things you've already done. This will point the way. And if you still can't do it you need to know you're not a failure just because you fail at one thing.

Though I struggled in some subjects, I loved Miss Rust's General Science Class because she recognized my ability to think. I could repeat most of that book to you today. Mrs. Kent taught mathematics. I don't think I ever did pass algebra, or if I did, it was because she was nice to me. But I loved ancient history. When I was 15 years old I made a working guillotine for French history with red ink on it all over the place. I didn't use any modern tools, just a sharp jack knife. If I needed a small piece, I whittled it. I also made a Greek warship with two rows of oars. The ship had a big sharp point on the bow the ship, which they used to ram and damage the enemy ships. I loved building things and it was so satisfying to find ways to apply that passion to my schoolwork.

Track

When I was a kid, if my dog Rex barked any place with a certain bark I knew he had something cornered and I would dash quick to where he was. Even though the ground was plowed I could run on uneven ground. If he had a woodchuck cornered he didn't dare touch it because the woodchuck sometimes bit his mouth. I would pick up a little stone and toss it and the woodchuck would lose focus, allowing the dog to get him. One time I ran back to the far woods. The dog was at the base of the tree looking up. A fox was up in the tree. I looked around and found a dead tree, broke off the roots and was able to dislodge the fox. It fell straight down, landed, crouched down low to the ground, taking off before the dog could get him.

Mr. Townley, the track coach, heard those stories and asked if I'd like to try out. We used to train on the Altamont Voorheesville Road behind his car. People made fun of my gait but that came from running across the plowed fields! I'm built like a runner and with a little training I did pretty well. So without bragging, nature had given me the stamina and the will and the wisdom not to get out ahead in a race, but to stay just back and look at the finish line and to estimate if I had enough of an energy burst to pass the other runners. So many times we would be ten to fifteen feet from the finish line and I would be just behind them and then sprint to the finish!

Moving on

At graduation, Mr. Townley, who was also the public speaking teacher, nominated me for the Declamation Prize and chose me to do one of the readings. Though I graduated by the skin of my teeth, I was proud to earn my diploma. One of the most important things I learned in high school was that it was possible to build my image of being from a good family. Whether they knew about my personal history or not, I made sure everyone knew who *Everett Rau* was. For many years, my mind worked to cover up my past and put on a good front. Funny thing is, I was looking at my graduation picture the other day. Of all those 32 people, hardly any of them are still alive. I daresay most were younger than me. At 96, I've read a lot of obituaries and am quietly thankful for good memories from so long ago.

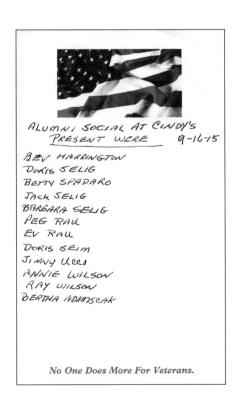

The Altamont Alumni Association

In 1954 the high schools in Guilderland were consolidated into one large high school in Guilderland Center. Altamont High School was eventually demolished and a new elementary school was constructed on the site, between Saint Lucy's and the Altamont Fairgrounds.

Over the years the alumni kept in touch with each other through the Altamont High School Alumni Association. Ev started attending meetings in 1986 and was president for a time. He enjoyed working with active members, Al and Helen Marion, among many others.

Besides hosting great banquets, the group raised thousands of dollars to fund high school graduation awards. In 1998, Annie Wilson came up with the slogan *$10,000 by 2000* and the campaign exceeded everyone's expectations. Today the Altamont Alumni Association still presents monetary awards to the top three Guilderland High School students.

Jack Selig has served as president of the association since 2006. Besides organizing social events, he has devoted himself to writing the history of the organization. With membership dwindling in recent years, the group decided to donate their records and photos to the Altamont Archives and Museum with a grant for preservation. Once they've been cataloged by archives volunteer and alumni association member, Virginia Ucco, they will be an invaluable resource for village history and genealogical research.

Left: Alumni meeting at the Home Front Cafe. Active members missing were Dick and Florence Ogsbury, Joanne Wagner, Bob Davenpeck.

1949 View of G.E. Building 81, the Turbine Division. Photo courtesy of the Library of Congress, Prints & Photographs Division, Gottscho-Schleisner Collection [reproduction number, e.g., LC-G612-T-45094]

Chapter 6

Observation, Common Sense, Reasoning

By the time I left high school, I felt like I knew everyone in the village of Altamont. Back then, people sat on their front porches in the warm weather and visited back and forth. I enjoyed stopping to chat on my way home from school in the afternoon. Everyone came out to the Masonic Hall for our school plays, which were the highlight of the week and were followed closely in the *Enterprise*.

Once I had some free time I started looking for work to help relieve some of the financial pressures on the farm. My first job was clearing brush in an orchard on the corner of Maple Avenue and Route 146 for Mr. Luther Warner, who became a friend of mine in Altamont. He recognized that I was a poor but outstanding young farmer who could use some extra income. He lived in the big house at the corner of Maple Avenue and 146 and had an old, unkempt orchard with a lot of brush and apple trees that needed pruning. He hired me in the spring of 1939 to rejuvenate the four-acre orchard into production. You can see it behind the house today, if you stand at Maple Avenue and 146. The property goes all the way back to the railroad tracks. It was hard, tedious work but I was used to that. My experience there shows that no job is unimportant because this one eventually lead to work at General Electric (G.E.), where Mr. Warner was an executive.

In the meantime I worked as a general go-fer at a used car lot in Schenectady, where I made a few dollars per day. I remember one time that the boss asked me to inflate some truck tires that they had just replaced. I refused because I'd heard that the tire's sealing rim could come loose from the wheel and that a kid had been killed inflating one. I told him that there was a cage they could set up as a safety measure. Well, he was pretty steamed and went to the owner and the next day they had a sturdy metal safety cage. I worked at the car lot for about a year and was lucky to be able to move on to G.E., in the fall of 1940.

Mr. Warner must have recognized something in me, during the talks we had at lunchtime, and when the job was finished to his satisfaction he asked me if I ever thought about working in the G.E. Company. It was a tricky little part in my life. I hesitated to answer him, because I had to build confidence that, having only solved farm problems, that I could succeed in such a large company. I suppose I had some fear of failure. But somehow despite the problems I'd overcome – both emotionally, and sadly with my father's misbehavior, I was able to summon up inner strength. So, hiding my initial fear of a big company and still questioning my ability to succeed, I mustered a smile on my face and with as much enthusiasm as I could generate, made eye contact with Mr. Warner and said, "Yes, I'd like to do that."

Eventually he suggested a position that included bookkeeping training and arranged for an interview. I was instructed to go at a certain time down to Building 1 where they conducted interviews with people looking for work. I drove over Weaver and turned left on Edison under the railroad tracks. There was an eight-foot high brick wall with the employment office. I opened the door and when I walked into the room, I thought this was what solitary confinement must look like. People were friendly in their businesslike way and I was hoping that they wouldn't see me shaking in my boots. There was a long line of chairs and two or three offices and I sat and waited my turn. Finally I walked in for the interview and filled out a lot of papers. I believe now that some word had come to them that Mr. Rau was going to come in. However at that time, my mind would have been unaware of any type of recommendation.

Even though my father and brother had worked there, no one ever talked about it, so the process was intimidating for a farm boy from six miles away, with no one I knew working at the plant. However, I was determined to present myself the best way my life had prepared me for, realizing I was now joining the competitive work world. They thanked me and told me they'd be writing a letter when there was an opening. We didn't have phone service on the farm until 1949.

Days were long, as I waited hopefully for a response. After a couple of weeks a letter did come, inviting me to a Building 2. I met with another gentleman, who said they'd been informed that I was a friend of Mr. Warner, who thought I was a candidate for a bookkeeping course. I signed up for one of the most frustrating things I've ever done. About the only thing I knew about figures was in grade school when we had to memorize the multiplication table from 1 to 12. I took algebra in high school, which I hated. I don't remember how long I went to the classes but I recall an interview where we talked about how I worked on the farm, what type of machinery we had, and what we did when things broke down. Somewhere in my life I've gained the ability to express both my accomplishments and failures honestly and directly.

The next week I reported to Building 81 and was put in a cage with all the blueprints and a nice young man, who was supposed to work with me until I could handle the job. This was one of the exciting parts of my early G.E. career because I caught on right away to reading the blueprints, which was a total foreign language to me. Every machine or part that was being manufactured had a blueprint, which broke down all the parts, so I could see each part and how they related on the blueprint. When I looked at the drawings, I knew which blueprints fit together because of working on the farm and taking machines apart. I also had an excellent memory for blueprint numbers, which was good because they had to be returned to their part number places every night.

The war effort didn't start with the bombing of Pearl Harbor. G.E. was already making airplane equipment for the war effort. Our department was building transmitter/receivers, which were very large radios that could transmit and receive. They were destined for B17s and B25s. It was interesting to me to see them being made. Each one was on a small cart that ran on a miniature railroad track. When they were completed they went to an area that simulated the vibration of an airplane flying and machine guns firing. It was a shakedown test and if they continued working they went directly to shipping department. If they failed, they were switched to another track to go through the line again and be repaired. Being involved in such an effort was really mind boggling to me at the time, and working on such different machines expanded my reasoning potential. It was a wonderful experience!

After a year or two I was transferred to another department. All parts in large manufacturing companies were produced by piecework. For instance, to make something as simple as a washer, you start with a long coil of flat stock that is run through a hand-activated punch press machine. It was a dangerous job. One day I had to see a piece of a finger left on the machine. The piecework workers had to load the machine, set up the dies, and run the machine. Then inspectors would approve the set up so they could run the order. Nowadays you'd order washers from a place that only made washers and it's all automatic – probably computer controlled.

Certain parts had to be manufactured by several different machines and my job was to coordinate the work. I worked at a huge console, a little like a huge organ console. There might be six little piecework vouchers for a particular part. A piece worker would come up and hand in the voucher they had for the work they'd done. I would give him another job and sometimes, being piecework, he would ask for an easier one because the previous job had been tough and time consuming. I don't know how in the world my head expanded to deal with the thousands of vouchers, but almost instinctively I knew the console and I was commended for being able to balance out the load to keep everybody happy. I suppose it was because, during my years in the blueprint room, I mentally recorded thousands of pieces. I just automatically knew the good paying vouchers and the poor paying ones.

One day, toward the end of the shift, a group came up and reminded me that I hadn't joined the union yet. They said, "You ought to join the union. If you don't, you probably shouldn't go out into the parking lot." I didn't want to join because I saw myself as an office worker, not a union worker, and told my supervisor, who walked out with me. I thank God for giving me the mental strength to go to work the next day and work with that same group like nothing had happened. I may have favored some with good paying vouchers.

After that, I was transferred to an electronics department. My group had a galvanometer. I didn't know it then and I still don't know for sure, but I think we were working on the secret Manhattan project. As far as workers were concerned it was a rush job for a power generating plant on Manhattan Island. We were measuring the resistance in electronic resistors to an accuracy that to this day amazes me. The gauge was in a semicircle in a room the size of my kitchen. You put the resister in and the gauge would swing around. If a "normal" galvanometer had 100 marks, this had 100 x 100. If the pointer came between two marks, you had to interpolate and write down every measurement and make sure it went into the proper box.

As a farm boy, being exposed to this type of necessary, exacting, almost infinitely small measurements was almost beyond my ability to understand. Very few people walked into that room. We were chosen people. And even though we were chosen we took a gamble because we never knew exactly what we were working toward. All we knew was that there was a broken power generator in Manhattan and it needed repair parts.

One of the other the highlights of my time at G.E. was when we were asked, one afternoon, to stay overtime without pay to go up on top of Building 2 and witness something new. Of course I was there. It was just getting dusk and they said it was *radar*. The radar sent out some type of wave which would bounce off buildings and come straight back. On the screen we were able to see the same buildings we could see by eyesight – exciting – especially for the farm boy that trimmed the apple trees and fixed the broken cultivator in his free time.

After that I became an engineer's assistant for a marine armament project in a super secret area. My job was to take any idea the engineer thought about or designed to do a job, test it, and to see if it worked. When not working directly with the engineer, I was also a production worker on a machine that made the parts that went into a secret battery.

In the room where I worked was a machine that had been giving them trouble for about six months. They were under pressure to get it working. Every day I'd see a new group of technicians come in to try and figure out why the machine wouldn't function the way the engineer designed it. This went on for several months. One day I was called into the office for a conference and the conversation went: "Mr. Rau, we know you don't have a college degree, but we have tried all the people we have available to make this machine work." I was introduced to the engineer who made the machine. They knew I had previously watched the machine malfunction and asked me what I thought was wrong. I replied that to me it was obvious that the pressure was so great that the rollers bend. The college-degree engineer who designed the rollers in a very loud and angry voice said, "The rollers do not bend. I designed and had them built. They do not bend!"

This timid man walked into a waiting room on a cold blustery day and didn't close the door behind him. A big burly guy got up, walked over to the timid man and in a loud voice asked, "Were you born in a barn?! Why didn't you shut the door?" The timid man started to choke up tearfully and looked up at the big burly man and said, "Yes, I was raised in a barn. And whenever I hear a jackass bray it makes me terribly homesick."

So they asked me if I'd be willing to give it a try. They were already six months behind on delivery to another G.E. plant in Springfield, Massachusetts. So the next day I ran the machine the whole day and got the same poor results. On the second day I watched it at the same time that it was rolling a sheet of malleable material. Most every time it would extend the outer parts of the material just a little farther than the center so the material would roll up and make a wrinkle in the center, which was unacceptable.

This is another time in my life where I feel I have to give credit to the super power that has helped me all my life. I studied this material, which was supposed to go through rollers and remain flat, and observed that the edges grew faster than the center. I somehow thought of my mother rolling pie dough to cover a pie. She would lay the piece of dough on the pie, only to find that it was an inch short on one side. I can picture it today. She would put the pie dough on the breadboard and use the pie dough roller and put a little more pressure on the side that had to grow. Then she would pick up the pie dough and put it on the pie and it was big enough to over hang and be trimmed off. I determined that the unequal pressure mother put on the pie dough to make it grow faster on one side than the other was exactly what was happening in the machine.

Another thought also occurred to me. Miss Rust was a general science teacher in Altamont High School, who was able to instill memorable ideas in my mind. The one thing that I remember that helped me do my thinking about this problem was that when you hold a magnifying glass level and turn it up on its side you can't measure the difference but the pull of gravity would very slightly alter the shape – ever so slightly. Through this I knew that in a very precise machine even the smallest bending or distance or pressure can make a difference when absolute exacting pressure is required to make the machine work.

So now I'd analyzed what I thought the problem was… How did we fix it? I knew it would be useless to ask the engineer to alter the rollers "because he designed them and they don't bend!" We were fortunate that there happened to be a stainless steel sheet beneath the malleable material. Figuring that the roller bent up in the middle to put more pressure on the edges, I went to the Material Parts Department and ordered shims to increase the thickness by one thousandth of an inch in the center to equalize the pressure. Inserting shims in the center made up for the bend in the rollers and allowed the roller to work flat. Just like pie dough. Much to my surprise and amazement, it worked!

I spent the rest of the day running the machine without a failure and did not tell the boss. At the end of the day I shut down the machine and went home. When I came in the next day I ran several sheets through successfully and told the boss that maybe I had the machine fixed. He said to be prepared at noon to make a demonstration. There was Navy brass there from Canada and from the U.S. Navy. They told me to run the machine. Needless to say, "this was the moment of truth." So I ran the machine. They said run another one, run another and another and another. The boss said, "Mr. Rau we've been working on this for six months and tried everything. What have you done to that machine to make it work?" I explained how I placed the shims underneath the steel plate to make up for the bend in the roller.

I call this my day in the sun. The engineer was present in the meeting, and I never saw him again. He had used all his doctor degrees and followed the book but didn't have hands-on experience. Though I felt triumphant, I recognize in retrospect, that there were more sophisticated ways I could have handled the situation. Here you have the engineer, frustrated that his machine's not working, in front of the big shots and some clown (me) says the roller bends. I could have fixed it and then told the boss, but I wanted to be 100% right. What's interesting is that the analogies come to you when you need them. I think the word intelligence is somehow related to the ability not to carry the burden of yesterday's mistakes but look to the future to be able to solve problems and be successful. There was no space for me to worry about whether I could do it or if I would fail. I always fall back on observation, common sense, and reasoning.

Later on I worked in one of the laboratories where they put a fountain pen in your pocket when you came in the morning. They would read it at noontime and it would say if you could work the afternoon or not. I always say that those extra radioactive atoms bouncing around in me is why I've lived this long.

My work at G.E. continued, even though the war was over and we were mostly doing busy work. I felt funny about doing such little, insignificant assignments. In order to get paid, the boss would verify that I had worked 40 hours even though I wasn't working much. There was apparently plenty of money to pay us and they didn't want to let us go just in case. Eventually G.E. made an arrangement with Rensselaer Polytechnic Institute in Troy to provide outstanding workers with scholarships and they offered me one.

By 1950 we had three children. We were raising a lot of turkeys and still raising pigs and selling pork and sausage. I feared that I would not be able to do justice to an RPI scholarship. After working all day, I would have to attend classes at night in Troy, which would have put me home quite late. Besides the long hours, I was worried that my father would misbehave with Mother and Peg if I weren't there to keep an eye on him. I remember coming home and talking with my wife. Given the slow pace of work at the time, I figured that by declining the RPI scholarship I would eventually get laid off. It was a difficult decision to give up the financial security and respect I had gained at G.E. but I felt compelled to balance that against the need to keep an eye on my father and the family.

When I gave my notice at G.E. they kept me in the office for half a day. Because I had a wealth of knowledge in my head I was interviewed by several people, including, I believe, some FBI agents. It felt like a cross-examination. Finally I prevailed and said no, I'm quitting to go into business for myself. They didn't like it but I quit.

"Standing Tall" Photo of Ev in 1943 by Peg Rau.

Top left: Frank Levey Vedder and Blanche Leotta Jeffords wedding photo.

Middle left: Grandfather Charles Vedder.

Lower left: Peg seated (middle) with girl-friends, Dora and Olive.

Upper right: Peg as a toddler.

Below right: Frank Vedder, Catherine (Dropper) Vedder and Peg's stepbrother Charles G. Vedder.

Lower right: Peg with friend Dora Staver at a G.E. picnic.

Chapter 7

Peg's Story

In 1942 I worked in payroll and accounting at G.E. My office had six big desks pushed together. There were two managers assisted by two women and two men. The woman next to me was the most capable, so she managed the cash window. Sitting at my table I could see the whole big office, and began to notice a man who would come past the office every day to punch in his time card. I thought he was good looking and asked my girlfriend next to me, "When he punches in, go out there and look a the time clock and see what his name is." I had a friend who worked over in his building, and when I met her for lunch, I saw him working the cash register, checking people out of the restaurant. Ev and I finally became acquainted when my friend told me she had to go to the hospital. Since she would be absent for some time, I would be giving Ev the clock cards for his office.

Our first date was at a gorgeous restaurant outside the city, toward Ballston Spa. A governor had lived there so they called it Governor's Inn. I had never been to a place like that for dinner in my life. Now that I was working I had new clothes, so I wore a nice dress and a beautiful big hat. Ev never liked big hats because his mother never wore them, so he always talked about my hat. He asked what I wanted to drink and, of course, I had never had any alcohol in my life. I said I'd have what he was having and this was the first time I tried scotch and soda. I did like scotch but preferred Manhattans to the daiquiris, which he loved. But that's long gone. After dinner he asked if I wanted to go to the movies and we went. I loved movies. I went every Thursday with my girlfriend when I was working. It wasn't until years later that I learned that he hated movies! I treated him to *Lawrence of Arabia* when it came out and all he did was criticize the effects — "That's just paint, not real blood." After that, I said, "No more movies for you. You're too practical."

Once we were dating he would walk me back to my office when he was through with his shift. We would stand and talk, and the girls would say to me, "How come you just had lunch over there and stood out there and talked for so long and now you're talking to him on the telephone!" We had both dated other people but we liked each other right away. We each had difficult childhoods and though I had grown up in the city, my

61

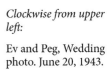

Clockwise from upper left:

Ev and Peg, Wedding photo. June 20, 1943.

Farmer Peg

Ev's mother (Mom) and Jim

Father, Rex, and Jim

Mom laying out patterns

Mom and Ev

Peg, Jim, Mary Jane, and Ernie

parents and grandparents had also been farmers. I knew right away that he was something special. We had our first date in August 1942 and were engaged at Christmas that year. We married on June 20, 1943 and moved to Ev's home on the farm in Altamont.

I was born at the Vedder family homestead on Pangburn Road in Rotterdam to Frank Levey Vedder and Blanche Leotta Jeffords. Though I spent most of my life in town, all my Vedder ancestors were from the farm. They were descended from the Amsterdam Dutch who settled here in 1637. We have a Vedder genealogy, which shows that they were here during the burning of the Stockade in Schenectady. The original family settled on the flats west of G.E. near where Rotterdam Mall is now. In fact, there's a little fenced off area near the mall where the cemetery is preserved.

My mother was Blanche Leotta Jeffords and she was from a big family in Schuylerville. She grew up on Church Street. I can remember going to that house as a small child. They had a kitchen that was down on the lower level. It was a nice home. I was tiny enough that I could take my nap on two chairs just under the dining room table. Her people fought in the Revolutionary war in the Battle of Saratoga. Though my grandfather was born on a farm, by the early 1900s he and his sons were working in mills along the Hudson River in and around Schuylerville. One of my uncles became an auditor for a big company and lived in India for a long time. Two of my aunts lived in Schenectady. My mother went to business school in Schenectady, where she lived with her older sister until she met and married my father.

Sadly, Mother died of tuberculosis in January 1927, when I was three. I'm sure this was a terrible blow to her family, who lost their son in 1923 and mother in 1928 to the same disease. I never knew what, but something happened to damage relations between them and my father. I have one very early memory of Christmas presents that my father would not let me unwrap because they had to be returned to the givers. He cut off all relations with the Jeffords family and threatened to disown me if I spoke with my aunt Stella in Bellevue and my aunt Frances, who lived right across the street from my high school.

Once I was married I would occasionally talk with Frances on the telephone. Either she called or I called her. One day, I talked to Everett's mother and I said, "You know mom, I think I'm going to go see her. I'm a married woman now and I can do what I want to. As far as disowning me he's done that anyway." She agreed to go with me and we had a nice visit. Some years later Frances called because she'd heard that my father was ill. She said she didn't care what happened to him – that if he was sick, he deserved it. Why? I'll never know because I never saw her again. She died before I had the nerve to ask what the feud was about. As a result I've never known my mother's family. I never knew how my parents met. I never knew anything about them.

Around the time of my mother's death, my father's family was moving away from farming. I never really understood everything that happened but at some point during my childhood the family farm was sold to Civitella's and then to the Overbaugh's. I always wondered why Grandfather didn't sign it over to my dad, who was an only child and had grown up there. Though one of my father's cousins lived on upper Broadway in Bellevue, the brothers of my grandfather, who had grown up at the homestead, were living up and down Duanesburg Road and one maiden sister up at Kelly Station, were all living in the hills where they had been born. We were very friendly with all of them, my father's cousins. In those days we had a lot of visitation. People would just stop in and call. They didn't call to see if it's okay. They would just show up. We were very close. Everett knows a lot of them too. Funny part was all those people live in close proximity to where I finally landed up, which was not far from where I was born.

After my mother's death we lived for a time in my grandfather's home at Edgewood Avenue in Rotterdam, then moved to the family homestead in Rotterdam, and when I was five, to my grandfather and step-grandmother in Scotia. They bought a house and I went to school at the Mohawk Elementary School, where I had four or five really good friends. There were lots of parties in Scotia: birthday parties, Halloween parties and parties at church. But though we were financially comfortable in Scotia with my grandparents, I was sad not to have a mother and frustrated with my grandmother's old-fashioned ideas. She was a devout Methodist and was very strict with me and with my grandfather. She had these quiet times if she didn't like something he did and it created a lot of stress for him and for me.

I had wonderful Christmases and I got beautiful gifts, but I always resented their old-fashioned rules. For example my girlfriend had a beautiful new bicycle but when I straddled it, pretending to ride, I got sent to my room. One day I went for a Sunday walk with a neighbor. Where did you go? We went to the park to watch a ballgame. I had to go to my room without dinner because we weren't allowed to enjoy ourselves on Sunday. My grandmother would never let me wear any kind of pants. Even in the snow, she made me wear those old fashioned black stockings and those god-awful buckle overshoes, so I wouldn't go out in the snow. If I had to wear them to school, I would shove them way down when I got there. Even after my father moved us to Rotterdam, I was still subject to my grandparent's wishes. I remember one day when I was about sixteen, I was wearing a nice pant suit that I had purchased with my babysitting money. It was a combination of overalls with a jacket in a beautiful shade of rose, very subdued. When I saw the bus come and my grandfather get off I rushed in to change so he would not see me in pants.

At one point we moved into one side of a duplex house that they owned on lower James Street in Scotia, where there was an alleyway connecting to Mohawk Avenue. Between our back yard and the barn was Colonial Ice Cream. The barn had originally been used for horses, but when we were there it was a rental garage. My grandfather always had a lot of trouble finding something to disinfect the barn so it wouldn't smell like horses.

My girlfriends and I used to play hide and seek. There were five of us and we used to play around the trucks at Colonial Ice Cream. I roller-skated from upper to lower James Street – all over Scotia. From where I lived, James Street comes into Ten Broeck. There's a big hill and at the bottom was a large concrete retaining wall, just high enough for people to stand or walk on it. The big challenge was to skate down that hill and not fly off onto Mohawk Avenue. If you could make that turn without falling off, then you could really skate!

In 1934, when I was 11, my father remarried and I went to live with him and my stepmother in Rotterdam. They were working at G.E. when they met, but she stopped working after they married. It was the Depression and when my father lost his job, she was very conscious of money and miserly with the things I could have. She hated having to make do with old things that had belonged to my mother and would make my father account for every penny he spent. If he didn't she would give him the business. This was a big change from the way things were with my grandparents. She hardly did housework, preferring to focus on her friends in the Democratic Club and card club. She loved to play bridge and read and read and read.

With my mother dead, my father and grandfather were the only ones I was close to. Unfortunately I never felt that my stepmother accepted me. My father was a very hard-working person, having grown up on the farm. While he was laid off from G.E., he delivered coal, where you dumped it down the cellar. He worked at anything he could get. Carpentry. Electrical. He could do any kind of work. I always tried to help out when he was working outside or fixing the car. I loved being a go-fer. Once he was called back to G.E. he worked nights.

When I was 15 my half-brother Charles was born. My stepmother was forty and had absolutely no idea how to take care of a baby. From my youngest days I loved children. I often visited my grandparents in Scotia and whenever there was a baby around, I'd offer to walk it. Back then they would let you walk their babies anywhere. They didn't know where that kid was. I was all over Scotia with that baby, even as far as Sunnyside Road because it was nice and calm — cool and peaceful. It was a very hot summer when Charles was born in June. He had colic. Constant crying, all the time. I did everything. I held him. I did his wash. One day my stepmother said, "If it hadn't been for you he wouldn't be alive." My dad gave me money and said, "Get on the bus. Go to a show. You need a break." He knew how hard I'd been working.

I got along with my stepmother alright until after Charles was born. Times were tough financially in 1938, but it bothered me that he could get anything he wanted but I couldn't have anything. I had one extra set of clothes. "You wear this today and that to-morrow," she'd say. I swore then that I would have nice clothes some day.

I started sixth grade at Draper in 1934 and went there until I graduated in 1940. I did fairly well in high school, though I didn't really like it. In the seventh or eighth grade they could skip you and they skipped me a half a year. When I got to high school she wanted me to take college prep courses even though she said there was no money for me to go on to college. She wanted me to do the Latin and French. I didn't do well in those. I wasn't a super student. Average, not above average. Of course I never felt that I was competent. I always felt I was below. She never built me up and always compared me to my brother. It's funny that I hated math, yet when I started working I used math in all my jobs.

I had wanted to be a teacher but she told me that I couldn't go on to college. "You'll be lucky if you can finish high school because you'll have to go to work because we can't afford to send you to college." We struggled over this and I remember one day she was going to take a chair to me – hit me with a chair! I said to her, "You know, if anyone asks me (my friends were always asking) how you treat me... from here on in I'm going to tell them I have no use for you. I don't care for you because you're not treating me well." She didn't say anything to that, but she did insist that I would have to leave school as they could not afford to have me continue. Since I graduated a half a year ahead of time, I was with the class ahead of me. I've never gone to my reunion because I knew very few people from that class.

My father was very bad when it came to going with people of the wrong religion or nationality. He'd go absolutely berserk. You don't go with that one and you don't marry such and such. Of course the Italian guy living next door to me thought I was wonderful. In fact, he happened to meet Everett at G.E. one time and Everett pulled out his wallet and the guy asked who the picture in his wallet was. Everett said it's my wife. "You married her! Her father wouldn't let me even speak to her." He was Italian and he was Catholic and that was enough. My father always had to know the nationality and religion for anybody I went with. When I heard Everett was Lutheran I was worried. Dad told a story of a friend who married a Catholic girl and when he came home one day he found the priest leaving after baptizing his child. Dad said his friend committed suicide. "You get on the South Schenectady bus," he would say. "What are they talking about? They're all talking about you. You don't know. If you get married your in-laws will be Italian. You won't know what they're talking about."

After graduating from high school, my stepmother suggested that I take a G.E. comptometer class. A comptometer is like a mechanical calculator or adding machine. They assured you a job if you passed the course. I first went to work in a dime store, but I did apply to the G.E. night school for the three-month comptometer course. I did so well that I was hired at G.E. before finishing the course.

My stepmother didn't like Everett and was never congenial to him. She would make little remarks to my father that Everett was trying to stay out of the draft, even though Everett had a special Class E deferment due to the secret war work he was doing.

Dad was working nights at G.E. by then and when I'd come home after a date with Everett my stepmother would have already gone to bed. At night she would undress by the heater vent in the living room and leave her clothes all over the room – underwear, corsets, etc. I would quick grab it up and throw it in the hallway when Ev came in. I don't know why he kept going out with me. A lot of men would say, I don't want any part of this.

My brother was five when I got married in 1943. My stepmother hadn't helped during the wedding planning and at one point I asked what color she was going to wear. She said something like "What does it matter? I'm not representing you at the wedding." "Then you shouldn't come," I said. "You'll make a fool of yourself sitting in the back of the church by yourself."

Thursday night, before the wedding, I took Ev's mother shopping in Schenectady. We were supposed to meet Ev at Proctor's Arcade, but when we got there he wasn't anywhere to be be found. Eventually Ev's uncle Clate showed up and told us that Ev had injured his hand at work. He had been trying to close a window in his office that was stuck. The glass broke and he cut a tendon, which meant that he got married with his hand bandaged and in a sling! Because of gas rationing, we couldn't make unnecessary car trips and worked it out that Ev would take my wedding clothes to the church in his car the night of the rehearsal. My bridesmaid stayed over that night, and after breakfast we took the bus to the church, where we dressed upstairs for the ceremony. When my stepmother came through the receiving line holding my brother's hand, I saw she had little tears in her eyes. I said, "Tears of joy, I expect." After the wedding, Ev's cousin, Reid Lainhart, drove us home in his convertible. We had canceled our honeymoon in the Adirondacks due to Ev's injury, but went up to Mirror Lake Inn at Lake Placid later that September. We went back up on our twenty-fifth and fiftieth anniversaries, following the same route.

Growing up without a mother I always felt alone in the world. So it was wonderful to be accepted so completely by Everett's mother. She had no girls and we bonded immediately. She never criticized me or put me down. Once we married, Everett didn't want me to work so his mother and I kept each other company. My stepmother had made fun of me when I brought home the apron I made in Home Ec. She laughed and laughed. So, when Ev's mother said I had to learn to sew, I said no, I'll do the knitting. But slowly she taught me to use the old-fashioned treadle sewing machine by the parlor window. She could make a dress from a pattern in two to three days. Over time I learned everything she could teach me. I remember once, having to re-do a collar three times before I could finally set it into the shirt. I got so frustrated I threw it across the room, but she said softly, "Just one more time." She also taught me how to hang wallpaper and to garden and to process all the food we ate — vegetables, fruits, meats, pickles, relish, cheese. We loved talking and working together.

Everett's mother couldn't have meant more to me than if she was my own mother. I know that when she died, I couldn't have felt worse, but I probably felt just as bad as Everett did. She's here all the time. She's here when we talk. She was so patient. So calm. Such a loving Christian woman. From the day I met her she was like that. Good Christian woman. I used to spend my weekends out here after I knew we were going get married. I didn't want to be home so I came out here. I slept with Ev's mother in her room.

My stepmother never visited, though my father did come out a few times. He could have been such a wonderful grandfather for my kids. He loved hunting and fishing. He knew carpentry. He made toys for Jim, my first one. He'd copy what he saw in the stores and give it to him for Christmas. Then one day he stopped communicating. She wouldn't let him come over or talk. Just before Jim left for Vietnam I called and said, "You'd better get out here if you want to see him." My dad did come out – and probably caught hell from my stepmother. He did write and Jim loved getting his letters in Vietnam. But I don't think he saw Jim after he came home. My daughter always believed that my dad did a big disservice to us by not standing up to his wife, but I felt that he did what he did to survive. After all, he had to live with her. I was here and I was fine. He knew I was fine. I could understand him.

Ev's and my marriage could not have been more different. From the earliest days we struck the word divorce out of our conversation. We didn't even use it in a joking way. When we had issues we worked them out. I remember early on when he said something and I reacted and he said, "You don't have to talk that way any more. You don't have to defend yourself." I try to tell the grandchildren that the secret to a good marriage is communication. You have to realize that you're two different people. You'll have to blend your personalities. Before you get married you can say almost anything you want, up to a point. You go home and the next day is a new day. But when you're married you have to settle it then and there. If you don't, when you get up in the morning it will still be there.

The Vedder family homestead on Pangburn Road, where I was born, is up on a hill. It's a beautiful old house that reminds me in many ways of this one. It, too, can be difficult to get to when the winter weather is bad, because you have to climb Knutti hill or Levey hill. I remember one day in 1929, when I was six, that I went to the farm with my step-grandmother. She said we were going to have hail, so we had to close the shutters or the windows would break. After we finished, we went out of the house and walked up a little road to a focal point at the top of the hill and looked right straight over to the Helderbergs, where we could see the sun breaking through the clouds on High Point near Altamont. I never dreamed I'd end up on a farm near there.

Chapter 8

Turkeyland

My advice to someone if healthy with a good wife and desire to improve financial income. Start some project small but set your goals high and be willing to apply your God-given ability and your good mind and work long hours and celebrate even small successes. –Ev Rau from a 1951 Schenectady Gazette *clipping about Turkeyland*

When Peg and I married in 1943 there was no inside bathroom at the farm. Peg recalls washing in the kitchen in the corner by the dry sink, when a neighbor walked in. Once the babies came, we bought a bathinette for bathing them. Peg trained the children to use our inside chemical toilet. I was happy that my kids didn't have to go down to the outhouse. though when they were older they loved to go there.

We had been carrying on farming the whole time I worked for G.E. We bought milk cows to supply milk for our growing family, raised veal calves, sheep, sold wool, broilers, and pigs. After Raymond left, I cropped the whole farm myself for a couple of seasons while working second shift. Mother and Peg preserved everything in sight, and sold flowers from her thriving flower garden. I used to take a washtub full of asters and gladiolas to the loading dock of Sears Roebuck in Schenectady, where they would transfer them into pots for sale indoors. While considering my future, I began selling pork sausage in the parking lot at G.E.

Turkeys had always held a special meaning for me, ever since my humiliating Thanksgiving in high school. When I began working for G.E., even at 50 cents an hour, I went over to Leland McClaine on Route 406, Giffords Church Road, and splurged on my first turkey, which mother stuffed and roasted. Back then when you bought a turkey you bought the whole thing. The guts were still in it. They took the food away from it for 24 hours before processing, so even though it still had intestines there wasn't much in them. It could hang a week in a cold room without getting anything inside (even flies). If you look at the markets in the movie, *A Christmas Carol*, the turkeys are hung with the heads on. When prepping the turkey we had to cut its feet off. I was so impressed with those great big feet that I dried them and kept them by the front door. I only wished I was back in high school to be able to say how tasty my first turkey was!

In the late forties we began raising a few turkeys to sell in the fall, and went around to the fire companies who were raffling turkeys for fundraisers. The biggest order was for 35 for the Westmere fire company, which repeated for several years. They liked our "Quality Products" because they were larger than the competition and looked really good. I bought three-day old turkey poults from Milford DeForest – a very fine Christian man. In those days he bred his own turkeys and through selective breeding had turkeys with really broad breasts. In addition, ours were really clean and nicely packed in clean heavy-duty tight-fitting plastic bags. Later our poults came from Leland McClaine, who selected toms and hens and artificially inseminated them, creating really superior stock. The neighbors knew I had to kill turkeys on such and such a night, and five or six would show up. If I had a dollar I'd pay them and if not, it was a fun time. Everyone was laughing and telling jokes. It was a reminder of the old romantic life in my boyhood days. No stress.

By the time I was selling them, people were really buying turkeys and Purina Feed was running a big promotion. The Purina representative came to me and helped with sanitation. He was an old-time sales rep and really took the time to help customers out. Nevertheless, come fall we had a terrific rainy October and every little barnyard impression allowed for standing water and I lost a bunch of them to weather and bad water. The next year I built a turkey ramp. It was over on the hillside to the east of the barn and was based on the design of the Cornell chicken coop. Ours had raised flooring – 1x2s with half inch spaces between them for drainage. We had four sections joined together to make a 48-foot, partly covered platform. Once raised off the ground the turkeys grew really well and we didn't lose a single one.

Our first child, Jim, was born in 1944, followed by Mary Jane in 1946 and Ernie, in 1948. Ken came along in 1957. My mother and Peg worked happily together and dad, for the most part, behaved himself. At one point he tried to talk to Peg the way he had to Mother but Peg's upbringing had given her a strong spine and she stood tall and he backed down. Still, it was enough for me to know that I couldn't risk being away from the house for work by day and school by night. Even though I was the sole breadwinner, Peg supported my decision to turn down the RPI scholarship.

I wasn't comfortable with such a light workload after the war and didn't want the embarrassment of being laid off, so I decided eventually to leave G.E. Given my successes there, I might have been a little bit conceited. In fact, giving that up was quite an emotional challenge, but I didn't let it stop me from figuring out ways to support my family and to make money. I don't recall what made me think of selling turkeys in town, or what motivated me to look for space and buy equipment. But once we had the idea, more ideas kept coming and I don't recall Peg expressing any doubts.

I do remember signing a rental agreement in 1951 with Mrs. Rosenberg for a vacant barbershop at 2533 Broadway in Schenectady. The new store was less than a mile from where Peg grew up and near the aging customers on my mother's butter and egg route. We bought a used glass-front deli showcase, three four-shelf pizza ovens, a 12 x 12 walk-in cooler, a meat band saw, and made work tables with good heavy linoleum tops satisfying the health code. Though linoleum was smooth and washable, we eventually wound up with stainless steel work tables. We made the letters for the Turkeyland sign in my cousin Kenneth Wemple's cellar on his band saw and officially opened the store on November 16, 1951. Though he was 78 by then, my father Frank was able and willing to help. We made a splash when we opened. There was lots of press coverage and I still remember seeing people lined up on the sidewalk at 9:00 a.m. on Thanksgiving with their roasting pans to pick up their roasted Thanksgiving turkeys.

Schenectady Gazette. November 14, 1952.

There was a supermarket across the street that sold turkeys for 59 cents per pound. When we opened the store I was selling my turkeys for 89 cents a pound. When people would call about my turkeys, I'd say yes I know theirs are less expensive. I used to raise turkeys that way, running on the ground. Ours are up in the air where their feet are clean and the floor is always clean. I had very few refusals when I gave them the sales pitch. I think you call all of that thinking – survival. But to get our price consistently, we decided to start catering. I'll never forget the time we got an order to barbecue 1,000 broilers for a Republican Party barbecue over at the Rotterdam Town Park. We bought the chickens, since we weren't raising that many on the farm at that point. It was a huge success and helped us gain confidence.

As I think back now I don't know how Peg and I rose to the occasion to do all this catering and we never made a mistake. Actually we did make one mistake. We took a job in the remote town of Summit, New York – over an hour away. We took everything we needed to the site from here. There weren't paper products back then, so we took dishes, plates, glassware. We had 100 cups, saucers, salad dishes, everything. Peg even thought of butter knives and knickknacks. We took it all. Things were going great until we realized that when we set up the buffet, we put the meat up *front* on the serving line. If you notice when you go to a buffet dinner, the meat is always at the end when guests' plates are full.

There was a type of ego nourishment that went with running the business. What

I really liked was the thousands of people who were steady customers. For years, total strangers would stop me and Peg on the street in Schenectady and tell us how much they loved Turkeyland. I can't get over the fact that I had no fear of failure. We were just so busy working that we never had time to be afraid. It was great working with Peg but it's a wonder she stayed with me. She had to do all the menial work. She was willing to do it because in her background you did what you needed to survive. But when it got to her, she let me know it! We both came from similar backgrounds. We might have been poor but we made out okay even though we didn't have surplus money. We didn't go without basic necessities but we had to work hard every day to get by. It's probably what drove us. We just moved forward. We went where the customers were, happy in our small store.

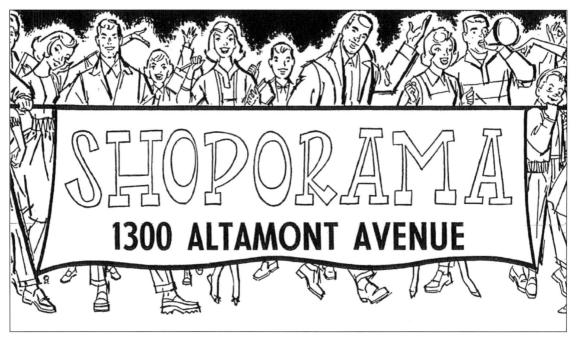

Shopping centers were just starting in the 1950s and Jim DeSantis, a big real estate man, and his partner, a Plymouth car dealer, stopped in at our store about 1953 or 4 and unrolled on the counter an eight-foot long elevation drawing of Shoporama, their proposed shopping center on Altamont Avenue in Rotterdam, where the Walmart and Hannaford Plaza are now. He had Turkeyland on the marquee. Having been a farm boy who worked in G.E., which built my ego to some degree, and then being super successful the first two or three years. . . . well all I can say is that my ego fogged my thinking. I told him it was a nice idea but I didn't have the money. They were so eager to have our store in their shopping center that they offered to help us out with a loan. This was probably the biggest mistake I ever made in my life.

The original Turkeyland consisted of Peg, me, a local man named Mr. Roosevelt and two or three girls. We eventually had 11 other girls. I used to spend the first half hour every morning listening to all their problems, while they got their heads on straight and ready to work. They were all old-fashioned, hardworking girls. They needed jobs. We paid them no more than we had to but we loved them and they all knew that and did whatever needed doing. One of our longest-serving employees was Hildegard Kery. Her son, Frank, was a bit younger than me and we spent a lot of time together as boys. She had moved out to the farm with her son to help mother with the summer boarders. When we opened Turkeyland at Shoporama she came and worked for us.

We opened the new Shoporama a couple of weeks before Thanksgiving in 1955. The new Turkeyland offered all kinds of meat. It was a self-serve delicatessen and a luncheonette where you could see your order cooked in a glassed-in kitchen in the rear of the store. We catered to organizations and made custom-cooked orders for busy housewives. Our store also offered exotic imported foods including European cheeses, meats, frozen foods, and ice cream.

One day, reading a trade magazine, I noticed a two-inch picture of a man standing by a bench with a boneless turkey roll. I think it was from the Chicago area. I stayed awake all night wondering how he did it. I realized that when you look at a skeleton, all the meat's on the outside of the bones. The next day I put the turkey up on the table and cut off the first and second wing joints along with the drumstick and then proceeded to skin the flesh from the skeleton in one piece starting at the back. As I got into it, it became obvious that this is the only way it could be done. I ended up with two half breasts and two thighs. All white meat on one side and dark on the other. I proceeded to cut it in half down the middle and reverse the pieces. I salted the inside and lined it up so the dark and white were opposite each other, tied it into a roll, cooked it and let it chill overnight. The next day I put it on a meat slicer and produced the first sliced turkey meat in Schenectady.

The turkey loaf was the start of a very successful and profitable and easy-to-make turkey dinner. We sold wholesale to Gibby's Diner in Quaker Street, Gershon's Deli in Schenectady, a deli in Rensselaer, one in Mount Pleasant, and two others in Albany. At Turkeyland, the turkey was kept refrigerated and when an order for turkey dinner came in we sliced off some pieces of cold turkey and put in a sieve, which was dropped into a pot of simmering turkey broth made by our good German chef Karl Godell from leftover bones. Turkey dressing was kept warm in the oven. We always had mashed potatoes, carrots or beans. A warm turkey dinner plate could be served in a matter of minutes before the invention of the microwave.

The turkey loaf built our business. When I saw that two-inch picture I envisioned the whole thing. There were 82 seats in our store at Shoporama. We were open 9 – 9, seven days a week. On Broadway we had raised our own turkeys but in the shopping center we bought from Swift and Co. because we needed them all year round. We had a glass case out front and sold all the parts: cooked hearts, livers, drumsticks, wings. They wouldn't sell today but back then they sold. And of course there was a tasty pot of soup on the kitchen stove simmering all day long.

You couldn't be in Schenectady with out knowing Everett and Peg Rau of Turkey-land were making headlines. One Thanksgiving WRGB asked if I'd be willing to carve a turkey on their TV program? I have no idea how I got up the courage to go on TV. My conscious mind said, "You idiot you're going to screw up." The other part of me said, "I can do this. I don't care who's out there. I'm just going to carve a turkey." When I later got famous for making up elaborate catering trays, I was asked to give a talk on how to do that on TV. We have a family joke about it. My wife will show me something with colors in it. "Too heavy over here. Like an artist." But you don't just make a flat tray. You put a brick down and put aluminum foil over it and then arrange the vegetables to give it height and eye appeal. You roll and twist the meat for eye appeal. I still can't believe I did this on tele-vision!

At some point the pressure started to get to me. My hands started shaking un-controllably and I was having a hard time sleeping. I don't know how I got past that. Dr. Grover fed me some kind of pills that straightened me out. Lord knows what they were but I spent quite a bit of money on pills until one day I made up my mind to stop taking them. I had some in the desk drawer. Closed the drawer. Two to three days later I stopped shaking. We had reached the summit.

The Shoporama management was big on special promotions. After we moved in, they arranged to have Johnny Podres come to the store. He was the winning Brooklyn Dodgers pitcher from the 1955 World Series against the Yankees. You can only imagine my ego. I didn't have time to worry about things, because at that point I had to get ready for Johnny Podres! You can't have too many mistakes that day. The store was packed. It was in the papers all over the place. I got a picture of Johnny Padres with me. That and a dollar and a half will buy a cup a coffee today.

Unfortunately, Johnny Podres didn't put much bread on the table. What you see now is a well-seasoned old fool! The rent was high. The electric was high. But the big-gest price my wife and I paid was to leave our three children with my mother and father, missing their childhoods for 10 years. Though I never wanted her to work, I couldn't have done Turkeyland without her by my side. Through all those years she somehow managed to celebrate Christmas, New Years and Valentines Day with the children, even though we didn't get home until 9:30 at night. Some nights, she'd walk upstairs and look at them in their cribs and cry. Looking back, it was was too big a price to pay for success.

In July 1957 construction began on the Altamont Avenue overpass, which effec-tively killed our Thanksgiving business that year. Car, truck, and bus traffic was detoured to Curry Road and Hamburg Street, cutting off Shoporama from the city. During construction our sales went from about $2,000 a week to $200, but our rent, insurance, and utilities stayed the same. We hung on by robbing Peter to pay Paul. My father had died at the end of 1955, right after the move. While I didn't have to worry about his behavior I worried that my mother was in her seventies and the primary caregiver of our children.

Mary Jane and Ernie with Grandmother Rau and "Gramma Cat." Early 1950s.

People didn't talk about work/life balance back then, but we were struggling with it. The early days, when the store was on Broadway were hectic, but manageable, because the store was only open 8 to 6. The move to Shoporama meant that we worked 9 to 9 seven days a week. With the increased catering and other pressures, there was a lot of stress on everyone. Though Peg felt like she was abandoning our children, they assured her that they were happy with their toys and the old barns and the open fields to walk in. Still, she must have felt some relief when the end finally came.

I remember in 1958 we had a huge snowstorm. One day it was sunny and the next there were ominous clouds and then snow. We could get home but I knew we wouldn't be able to get back to the shop if we stayed the night. So we brought groceries home for mom and the kids and then we drove back to Schenectady with our youngest son, Ken, and stayed with a friend of ours. Once the snow stopped we had 25-30 mile per hour winds for five days. They would plow the snow and it would just drift over. There weren't many cars on the road at the time, so the roads into Altamont were one lane wide. If you met another car coming, one or the other of you would have to back up. Route 397 was closed and we felt terrible that we couldn't get home to our kids for five days until a bulldozer finally pushed through the drifts, which were 6-8 feet high.

I'm sorry to admit that I enjoyed being a celebrity until they pulled the rug out from under me. I was constantly trying to think of new ways to gain customers. We ramped up our catering business to try and balance out the highs and lows in the restaurant. One memorable job was for the Millbrook Bakery opening on Fuller Road in 1959, where we deboned, tied, roasted, and sliced fifty 30-pound turkeys. Everyone was making sandwiches using Millbrook bread to hand out to people touring the new plant. We were still making sandwiches when the big bread truck backed up to the shop to receive the order! It was exhausting but we did it!

Even with catering we couldn't keep up with the expenses at Shoporama. When they finally asked us to leave, we opened at another location right near the entrance to the shopping center but it was too far for people to walk to get lunch. And there were more shopping centers competing for the same business. In retrospect, if we'd stayed in our original location on Broadway we'd probably still be there today.

I was so busy that I didn't think I was worshiping myself, but once the bottom fell out I had a hard time readjusting. To be on TV and then to be on the street with no business is not easy. We had expanded too quickly, but were holding it together until the bridge closure detoured traffic away from the shopping center. But unlike some of the larger stores, we didn't have any reserves to get us through. When the store was failing a nice local man from the IRS allowed me to get away without paying any FICA. I didn't pay FICA for a year. At some point his boss looked over his shoulder and really put the screws to me. I would have closed anyway but they put a padlock on the shop and locked me out. Part of me still thinks that some of the bigwigs downtown wanted to see the shopping center fail because it was a threat to the downtown merchants.

When we finally closed in 1961 we owed about 30 grand. I cashed in every insurance policy I had. I collected money any place I could. The big manufacturers took their machinery back so I considered us square. They took the coolers, refrigerators, air conditioners. I didn't have any guilty feeling about them because it didn't directly affect the salesman. But the butcher, the baker, the candlestick maker all got paid. I don't know how. Then one day I came home and found a letter ordering me to appear at the IRS in Albany. I was met by what looked like a 16 year old boy sitting behind the desk. "Well, Mr. Rau, I know you have trouble but we have to have the money by December 23 or we'll put you and your family on the street." I rolled up my sleeve and said in a loud voice, "You know sir, you remind me of what it must be like to live in Russia. You know what? Instead of setting my children out in the street, why don't you take my left arm. Cut it off. I'll give it to you!" They gave me an extension and I talked to a friend who referred me to an attorney and he got a delay. He asked if I had any land along the road that I could sell. We sold three lots in the woods and one across the road for anywhere from 1,000 to 1,500 dollars. Then I got in trouble with the Guilderland zoning board. They said I was making a development and I'd have to have my whole farm surveyed for $10,000. I just didn't have it. Somehow they let it pass, recognizing that it was still a farm.

One day, toward the end, I just had to get away from the store and come back to stand on the soil. As I drove over the Thruway on Route 158 toward home, I'm sorry to say I thought of suicide. It almost makes me cry to think about it even now. What was the point, I wondered. I was born, but what is my purpose in life? I had loved serving people at the store. And now it was as if I had wandered into a deep ravine and wasn't sure how I could ever climb out. As I pulled up to the farm, I could see the distant Green mountains and the sloping fields full of grain. The sheep were walking across the dam by the pond and our dog Rex came running over to greet me. I closed my eyes and lifted my head to the sun, and I believe God helped me to realize that I was here to father my children and care for my wife and my mother. I believe now that God gives us life for a purpose. Do not waste one moment. Get over it. Do not worry about tomorrow. Each day has enough trouble of its own.

Chapter 9

Thinking about Father

Growing up I had so much bitterness toward my father that I spent most of my life trying to compensate for the shame and resentment that was always simmering in the background. One of the blessings of a long life is that you have an opportunity to rewrite your own history as you gain wisdom over time. In the course of writing this book I've learned more about my father's life – things I never thought to ask when he was alive and it's beginning to allow me to see him as a man, rather than the bogeyman of my childhood.

My Rau grandparents immigrated to America in 1869, the year they married. They moved first to Schenectady and then to Syracuse. My grandfather Rau was a gardener and died when my father was thirteen. Dad and his brothers were forced to leave school to help support the family. But despite the tough start, Dad was determined to live a different kind of life. He began working as a commercial traveler (salesman) in 1899 and moved to New York City. I wish now that my mind was not so clouded with resentment at his behavior that I could have listened to the stories he told about that time. In the 1900 census he was living at Mills House No. 1, a hostel for poor young gentlemen at 160 Bleecker Street in Greenwich Village. The 1500 tiny rooms were closed by day to encourage the men to look for work. His neighbors included every type imaginable: authors, stock brokers, coachmen, a mining engineer, speculators, insurance brokers, lawyers, etc. He also exhibited in a YMCA Sketch Club show in Brooklyn in 1899 with other members of his YMCA evening art classes.

I do remember Dad telling adventure stories of traveling across Texas and the southwest as a hobo in his early twenties. He described how there were certain brake bars underneath the trains that the hobos could crawl under, and how some nights it was so cold they would pack their clothes with cast-off newspapers to keep warm while they slept. One time, traveling through New Mexico, a gang of kids was throwing rocks at the car they knew held hobos. One of his companions, a Mexican guy, took out his revolver but Dad convinced him not to use it on the kids – judging rightly that it would create worse trouble. I can still remember this poem that I learned from him:

Top left: Portrait of Father taken in Syracuse in 1905.

Top right: When a pig reaches a certain point in its breeding cycle it will stand perfectly still. Here is a rare picture of my father clowning around.

Middle right: Father on the farm with Rex.

Lower left: Father showing a barn owl to Ernest and Raymond.

Bottom right: souvenir silhouette postcard to Margaret Rau from Quinn's Fountain in Schenectady.

Guy comes down the road and comes into a tavern. Let me sit down a minute Cap'n. A stone's got in my shoe. Oh, don't commence your cussin. I ain't done nothing to you. Yes I'm a tramp. What of it? Folks say we ain't no good. But tramps got to live I reckon, though some folks don't think we should. Yes I was a blacksmith Cap'n. Eh, and a good one too. Way down the Lehigh valley, me and my family grew. Just me and my wife and Nellie. Nellie was just 15. She was the prettiest creature the valley had ever seen. One day there came this city creature. Dark and handsome and tall. Damn I wish I could see him strangled against that wall. He was the boy for Nellie. Nellie could see no ill. Mother she tried to stop em, but you know a young gal's will. One day they eloped together. Three days later they found her. Back to her home, they brought her, back to her mother's side. Filled with a raging fever she fell at my feet and died. That's when I took to drink Cap'n. So give me one more and I'll be on my way. And I'll tramp and I'll tramp till I find that scoundrel if it takes to Judgement day. (Anonymous poem popular at the turn of the century.)

One cold, clear night when I was little, Dad came in and told me to quick put on a jacket and come outside. Standing by the back porch, looking out over the hills that descend from the Helderberg plateau to the Hudson, I could see the double railroad bridge that crosses Route 20 down by Fullers Station Corners. The train that was crossing in the crisp, still, cold darkness seemed to be alive with fiery sparks. But Dad didn't just admire the scene, he explained to me how the engine worked. There was no air moving that night and when a train is under load the smoke and steam go out through the big smoke stack. This created automatic draft to burn the coal faster and hotter. You could see the steam and smoke going back over the train but then every once in awhile it would turn red when the smoke reflected the red-hot fire. The fireman had opened the boiler door, my father said, and shoveled in more coal. This was because a steam engine had to have more coal if it was under load. As I write this now I recognize this moment as a kind, fatherly act.

Though he was born and raised in Syracuse, Dad asserted in each census, from 1900 on, that he had been born in Colorado. Is it possible that being forced to quit school after eighth grade when his father died, that he was looking for something more out of life? Had he seen the soaring mountains on his hobo travels and felt reborn? Was he trying to distance himself from his German origins? Or perhaps he simply made a joke with the census taker in 1900 and then feared that changing his birthplace would have consequences later on.

I believe, based on their relaxed expressions in photographs, that my parents were happy together in Schenectady. And at 96, I can look back and see father as a man whose hard-won dreams were shattered by circumstances beyond his control. But as a teenager and young man it was all I could do to keep from harming him because of the way he treated my mother. And because I believed that everyone in the small, tightly knit community knew of our family's shame, I felt a tremendous need to rescue the Rau name and to prove to the world that I was better than my beginnings.

Memories of the abuse made it impossible for me to connect with Dad, even as he proved to be a better grandfather than father. Despite the fact that he could be bitter and controlling, I still remember many lessons he shared about nature and the world. When Peg arrived in 1943, my parents had settled into a kind of détente. Neither spoke much to the other, but both were welcoming to Peggy. She remembers him as incredibly tall and handsome, but very proud. She said he was isolated, living in his own little world and lashing out if anyone dared interfere. It was his way or no way and nobody dared cross him.

Peg felt he was wonderful with the children and we never could have embarked on the Turkeyland adventure without the solid support of both parents. If a child was fussing while dinner was being prepared, Dad would walk him or her around, showing off the pictures on the wall, and keeping them occupied until everyone was ready to sit down. I still recall the time our firstborn son, Jim, was bundled up and sleeping on the porch, on an especially chilly day. Dad came in from the barn and noticed a bit of exposed skin that didn't look right. He brought the baby into the warm kitchen, where Peg unwrapped him and realized that he wasn't right. Dad pressed Jim's chest gently a couple of times and when the doctor came he confirmed that Dad's quick actions had saved Jim's life.

But though he loved his grandchildren, Peg believes that when my father died it was just a matter of time before the kids would begin to test the rigid boundaries that he had laid down. Dad had a studio of sorts where he would work with his airbrush paintings in a small structure that had once housed the egg incubators below our house. He collected all sorts of little treasures, such as old nail polish and perfume bottles and tin cans. The studio was off limits to the children but Jim and Mary Jane admitted as adults that they used to go snooping down there when they knew no one was looking.

An act of kindness is good for both the giver and the receiver. One day, the summer before my father died, he asked me to drive him to the top of Settles Hill Road to see the sunset. I still remember his look of emotion as the panorama came into view. The timing was just right. The golden sun's last rim at day's end sank into the distant green hills. The flaming red and orange clouds and songs of the birds, along with the gentle westerly breeze gently tickled our senses with a caress that only God can give. As the evening gathered, I turned the car around without a word, and drove home. We heard my mother ring the bell for supper and Dad said, "That sure was a colorful sunset." After supper I slowly walked through the rustling fields of grain. The evening shown brightly in the western sky and one day ended to be followed by another day on the farm. It was two days before Christmas, 1955 that we got a call from the nursing home that Dad had died.

Closure

One day, fifteen years after my father's death, I was home alone. I went up to the big west room, which was full of boxes and papers, and noticed a stick frame book (portfolio) made of canvas. Inside I saw a charcoal picture of my grandmother and stacks of drawings. My father was a pretty good photographer and also had the ability to take a piece of charcoal and draw with such liveliness that you would almost hear a voice coming out of the portrait. Seeing these beautiful drawings — especially a spring photo of apple blossoms where he had airbrushed the colors so naturally that I could almost smell their perfume — I started to recall the way he introduced me to nature, to bugs, and trees. Then I saw a drawing of a painting of the Ascension, like the one on the wall in back of the altar in St. John's Lutheran in Altamont. As I examined the drawing a gush of Christian love came over me and I started feeling like warm water was flowing over my whole body. And from that day forward I found it easier to understand others – realizing that there's no point in carrying grudges. It's their life and their problems, not mine.

Drawn copy of the Assumption. Hand-colored photos of Ray and Ernest in Schenectady and Lainhart Road.

As I think back now, I believe my father wanted his children to grow up to be decent people. But I had a hard time recognizing the good mixed in with the bad. Even today I don't understand it, but I've come to recognize that nobody, not a single person, is all bad. It is sad to think he died alone in a nursing home in the total poverty of not having a loving family by his side. It's sad to see such a wasted life, which could have been so beautiful and full of love and respect. In retrospect, my dad was probably reluctant to give up a good paying job in G.E. to take over a working farm with sixteen-hour work days instead of eight. I wonder how he lived with the memories of his son Ernest who had died just as he was leaving for a bright future. I often think back about my father's total life. Hobo. Artist. Married. Seven children. Lost four. Not kind to my mother. Yet when I was a man with three children, this man who I saw smash the glasses on my mother's face helped me in my impossible dream of opening the store.

Artwork by Frank E. Rau

Quote reads: Art is to (sic) dim for eyes to see or heart to know. The future lives before us as we go. From childhood's dreams to life's reality, from days to years and then eternity. 1915.

Chapter 10

Perseverance

Our children grew up in a totally different world than mine. It was like the difference between white and black paper. They grew up in a family of love. In the early days, Peg stayed home while I worked at G.E. She threw herself into child rearing and farm work, helping Mother, who she called *Mom*, with the chores. Peg embraced farming and laughed as she recalled, "We picked beans all the way from here to Altamont. One November day, Frank and I picked field corn together. I was pregnant with Ernie. It must have been 35 degrees outside. I was big as a house. He was a 10-pound baby and by then all I could wear were oversized coveralls. I just couldn't get warm." Peg learned to drive the steel wheel tractor and helped plant the plantation of Scotch pines in the Quarry lot. But more than anything, she appreciated Mother's infinite patience and Christian guidance.

We both survived difficult childhoods, which gave us strength and determination to make a different kind of world for ourselves and our children. As my world expanded at G.E., Peg's opened out in different ways at the farm. Though her girlfriends couldn't believe she had given up the conveniences and bustle of city life, Peg focused on the flowers growing all around the house and the love and acceptance she felt from my mother. I don't think she would have stayed with me if it hadn't been for my mother! When one of her girlfriends asked how she could stand being out in the remote countryside, where it was so silent and dark at night, Peg said, "If I want lights I can stand out back and see lights all the way to Troy. We like it here, away from the noise and confusion."

Having the children safely ensconced with my parents also gave Peg unusual freedom for a mother in those times. She didn't have to worry about babysitters if she wanted to see friends or go to the market. We became more involved in the Grange, taking on leadership positions of increasing importance. We could go to meetings together, knowing that my parents were there for the children. And of course, having them there allowed us both to devote ten intense years to the store. My father passed away the year we moved to Shoporama and Mother died in 1962, about a year after the store closed.

Unfortunately, when the store closed, I descended into a two-year depression that

I still have a hard time describing. Going to town was torture. Because of TV, Peg and I had become such fixtures in Schenectady that total strangers would greet us on the street. I was so ashamed at losing our business that when I did go out I would cross the street to avoid talking with old customers or acquaintances. Farming was a solace, but the anxiety, guilt, and stress created health problems that seemed to swamp me in a kind of malaise. We were heavily in debt and the farm was not self-sustaining. At my lowest point, Peg suggested that we return to St. John's Lutheran. There I heard the message of hope from Reverend Keene Hilton and his caring wife, Marge, and began to heal.

Peg never badgered me about my condition, but one day after breakfast she stood up and said, "Well, you never wanted me to work but somebody has to have a job around here." She contacted an employment agency in Schenectady, thinking she would go back to the dime store she worked at in high school. When there were no openings, she applied to Wallace's Department Store. Peg was offered a job starting the day before Thanksgiving, taking pictures of Santa Claus with the kids.

According to Peg, "I remember thinking, well this is going to be different, all right. I took the pictures and another girl was in charge of the money. We worked together until one day the girl who was handling the money didn't show up for work. The money disappeared and people weren't getting their pictures. It was a mess. The manager came to me and they said, from here on in you're going to do both jobs. Because Santa Claus got paid for every picture, he insisted that all the kids get photographed, whether they wanted to or not. After all, he got paid even if the child was screaming.

Once the holidays were over they wanted me to work full time in the Men's department in the basement. At Wallace's they wanted you to be busy all the time, but there wasn't enough to do. Everyone had to fold and refold and refold. I needed to do something other than folding and refolding all day long, so I went back to the employment agency and took an aptitude test. My aptitude was all math, of all things! Of course I'd had all that in the store, where I was constantly working with figures.

On all the interviews, like Schenectady Savings Bank, they wanted to know what I would do if the store reopened. Would I be going back? Also my mother-in-law wasn't too well. Would I be going home to take care of my kids? Eventually they sent me to Schenectady International. I had known the big boss there from the store, so he was familiar with the name and all. He wanted to know if I was going to go back to the store. I told him I wasn't feeling it would reopen, so he hired me right away in the accounting department and I worked there 26 years until I retired in 1988."

Mother's Passing

My mother's health had been in failing for awhile and she died in July 1962 at the age of 81. It was a sad time for the whole family, though I'm more philosophical today. She had a good long life and was able to die on her own terms. She had gone upstairs to bed and we called the same doctor who had delivered our children. He came and talked to her and checked a few things, like her pulse. When he came downstairs I told him that she wasn't eating and asked what could be done. "We can take her over to Ellis Hospital and they can put her in an oxygen tent," he said. "She always wanted to die at home," I replied, and he agreed. With the doctor's support, we chose to keep her comfortable at home.

That night she asked for a pencil and paper and tried to write down the Christmas presents she had made for each person. She couldn't write clearly enough, so with great emotion I wrote down "gray skiing mittens for Ernie, pretty scarf for Mary Jane," and so on. After that, she lay without talking for a day and then suddenly sat up and asked, "Where am I?" I told her she was at home, in her own bed and pointed to the window and the hedgerow of her childhood. "Oh yes," she said and laid back down without another word. After a little while she wiped her forehead with a tissue and her arm relaxed on the bed. We watched as she took a couple of big breaths and went peacefully to the Lord. We all hugged and cried tears of sorrow for awhile and then, with regimented authority, I called the funeral home in Altamont. Thus ended the life of love for her children complete with abuse from my father. Mercifully she had nine years of peaceful love and kindness, especially by Peg, our family, and countless friends.

Peg missed my mother terribly and because she was working, she had to scale back on some of the things they had done together. According to Peg, "I would get the meals, clean up. Sew all evening. I made all my clothes. When the kids were small I made all their clothes, too. I made Mary Jane's wedding gown. I did the painting and wallpapering. I didn't have time to do any gardening until after mom died. But the day she died I walked around the yard. She had flowers all over. It was very hot. I thought, I guess it's up to me to learn to take care of these flowers. That's when I learned how to garden."

Hypoglycemia

About this time there were a couple of scary episodes when I experienced uncontrollable anger. The first time I was working in the sheep barn helping a newborn lamb to nurse when I bumped my shoulder on a sharp spike. It hurt so much that it triggered a surge of adrenalin and I picked up the sheep that had just given birth and tossed it across the barn in a rage. I think back on this with anguish. This was not me. I was trained to help, not hurt. I loved animals and my rational mind can't imagine doing anything like that. The next time, I was in the basement, putting wood into the big furnace when I singed my arm. I picked up a piece of wood, ready to clean everything out (including the furnace). It was like I was on a rollercoaster and couldn't control the adrenaline rushes that took over.

That second incident was on my mind when we were shopping at the health food store. I really wasn't feeling good. As we waited in line to buy our raw grains, I noticed a little booklet next to the cash register, *What You Always Wanted to Know about Hypoglycemia*, for $1.00. When we got home I realized that I had over half of the 15 symptoms on the list: sweaty palms, nervousness, short temper, and others. The author suggested a cleansing diet of raw beet juice. Of course my loving wife nearly drowned me with beet juice! She also put me on a high protein, low carb diet. Before leaving for work she would cook a breakfast of meat and lots of cantaloupe and soon I began to feel better. I just thank God that we caught it in time before I had any noticeable damage to my pancreas.

I never went to a doctor. The pamphlet had a clear description of how sugar works. Your body has the means to store some sugar – it's the fuel that runs your body. When you eat sweets, your sugar goes up and then the body brings it down below where it should be. This was clearly the teeter totter that I was on. It was such a relief to know that I wouldn't react if something happened while I was standing next to my wife. It was horrifying to think that I might become an abuser like my father, with no way to control my temper. The Lord has sure helped me to be here today.

About a week later I felt pretty good. It had been three weeks since I had to stop cutting hay early because my breath had been really short. Now I decided to walk down through the field the easy way, across the bottom and then back up the hill. Walking up I noticed that I had to stop a couple of times, but when I would breathe my energy would come back. A few days later I was cutting hay and my neighbor Earl Gray, the thresher man, stopped his car and walked across the field. "I noticed you started this field and you quit," he said. "What happened?" I don't know whether it was love or inquisitiveness but I appreciated the neighborly concern. I finished baling the hay on the rest of the farm. The weather was with me as I worked alone, cutting, raking, baling, loading the wagon and stacking the bales in the barn. I worked slow but steady, resting now and then. Survival.

Finding my voice

After the store closed, I struggled every day to face myself in the mirror and try to think of ways to move forward. The first concrete lifeline I found was from Dale Carnegie's book, *How to Win Friends and Influence People*, which made so much sense to me and included many suggestions that we had been doing in a less professional way at the store. Someone mentioned a sales training course and, coincidentally, an acquaintance, John Heron, was a trainer in Colonie. I took the course and then decided to work for him – traveling with a classmate to various villages in the area to sign people up. The sixties and seventies were tough and people really needed the help. We would rent a room with chairs and a podium and teach the five-day course. We went down to Millbrook, put up signs around town, rented a room and conducted a number of training courses. It was exciting and would have been my very first job after the store.

Toastmasters was another organization that made a difference for me at the time. I had been going to meetings while I was working at the store and continued on after. At Toastmasters you go for dinner with 20 – 30 people. Under your coffee cup is a slip of paper. After dinner, when it's your turn, you turn the cup over and look at your note. You have 30 seconds to think about the subject and 60 seconds to talk. Then they critique you. How it trains the mind to think under fire! Going back after the store closed I realized that I had lost the store but I hadn't lost my voice.

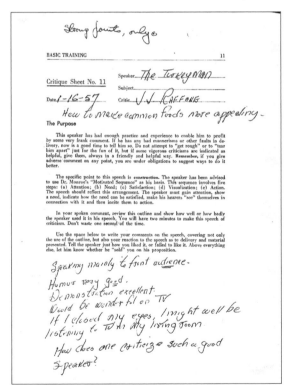

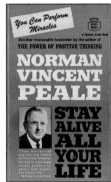

Left: Toastmasters critique of Ev's presentation: *How to make common foods more appealing. Top right:* Two of the dozens of self-help books that Ev used as resources. *Bottom right:* Ev worked as a technical sales rep for a company that sold and serviced commercial laundry equipment. While at Turkeyland, he learned to make ice sculptures and produced two shirt sculptures in ice to celebrate the opening of a commercial laundry in central New York.

Eventually I began pulling myself together. That's when I looked at the want ads. There weren't many jobs that fit my skills directly, so I started following up on all the sales jobs in the paper. I realized that if you want to become a good salesman, you should answer as many sales ads as you can. Go for the interviews and see how they try to convince you to work for them. I laugh when I think of some of the approaches they have. The products they were selling weren't worth a bag of beans but I learned so much from their pitches!

To get my first real job after the store, I walked into a large room in a motel in Menands. It was packed. I don't have a chance, I thought. They don't know me. So I sat up front and wrote down a couple of questions during the presentation. They must have been the right ones because I got hired. The boss must have liked my style of selling, because he asked me to talk to a group of thirty or forty new sales people. Now I had never, ever thought of sales training, but I decided to use what I learned in Dale Carnegie. Use and know the product. Make friendly answers to all questions. And if you're asked a question and you don't know the answer, simply smile and ask why the customer asked that question. Wait a brief time. If there's no answer, ask did they have a bad experience with the issue they raised? If still no answer, you will have had time to relate one of your own experiences and move on about the product. After many questions from the group I closed the training session with this very important sales point: *Do not allow anything to distract you from making your sales pitch.* While talking behind the podium I was able to unbuckle my belt and adjust my pants so when I walked out from behind the podium — talking about not being distracted — my pants fell to the floor — all the while talking about not letting anything get in the way of your sales pitch. They probably could not hear me then, but I made my point. Too bad the product didn't succeed.

That job didn't last long and I had several sales jobs after that. Though I had friends across the state and enjoyed the community of other sales reps who collected in small town diners, I hated spending so much time on the road. In one job I drove over 1,000 miles a week. A few nights I found myself jolted awake as the car bounced over rumble strips, heading for the concrete bridge abutments on the Thruway. There's a higher power up there and if he's not paying attention, I realized, you could end up a statistic!

Besides the long hours, I also didn't approve of the business culture of the time. One company, I felt, came close to the line when it came to special "customer bonuses." Keeping the sales reps happy once involved hiring escort services at sales conventions. And in a different company I found myself being used to drive my boss to dates with his mistress. Long hours drinking with customers rolled into long drives home and it took my high school-age son Ernie to set me straight.

The company I worked for at the time gave me a paycheck and traveling expenses and, though it's hard to imagine today, they gave me $100 per week to spend on the customers for booze. One night I came home from Schenevus, about an hour from Altamont. I'd had six boilermakers. A boilermaker is a shot of whiskey and a beer. My son Ernie, who was still in high school, was sitting at the kitchen table when I got home, smoking a cigarette. I said in my slurred speech, "You shouldn' be smoking, iss not good for you." He looked at me and said, "Dad, we love you. Your drinking isn't good for you."

Though I didn't react at the time, his words kept coming back as I tried to sleep that night. When I went back the next day to the same customer, he said, "Ev, it's time to quit." We went to the bar. I ordered a drink for him and a ginger ale for myself. Two weeks later, when I got into the office the secretary said the boss wanted to see me. "Mr. Rau, I understand that you're not drinking with the customers. Your sales are going to go down and we'll have to fire you." There was a performance list on his desk and my name was about half way down. I looked at him and said, "My name will be on the top of that list." A few months later, when I had climbed to the top of the list, I went into the office and asked to see the boss. When I walked into his office he patted me on the back. I took control of the meeting and said, "Let's sit down. I'm giving my two-week notice." He got up from behind his desk and walked over to me and asked what was wrong. I said, "I never wanted to be fired so I'm giving you my two-week notice." He said "You're doing fine. Don't worry about it." "No," I said, "I'm giving my notice, I quit."

Finances continued to be a challenge, even as the kids became independent. At one point, some people approached me about putting a cell tower on my property. It was a perfect location for relaying signals from one tower to the next and would have greatly improved service in Altamont. They were offering $6,000 a year, which would have made a huge difference to the farm at the time. Though set back in the woods, the tower would be 110 feet high and a balloon test showed that it would be 20 feet above the mature trees.

There were a number of town meetings, and I chose not to attend the final one because I was too emotional and knew I would not be able to control myself. Our near neighbors submitted a petition with eleven names, saying that they had no problem with the proposed tower. Unfortunately, the people farther up Settles Hill Road and the surrounding area argued that the tower would impair the view. One of my neighbors stopped by after the meeting to let me know how it came out. I'm ashamed to say that after he left and Peg went to bed, I lost control and smashed a chair. By then I was in my eighties and had been diagnosed with prostate cancer and was struggling to see how I could leave the farm intact to my children. Somehow, despite the disappointment, we muddled through and we're here today, thanks to the love and support of our children.

Children

Thinking of it now, the loss of the business, followed so closely by my Mother's passing, must have been challenging for our kids. Jim was 18, Mary Jane was 15 and Ernie was 13 and Ken was just 5. With Mother gone, Peg working, and me on the road, they would have grown up quickly. When I was home I always tried to share what I knew about farming and mechanics with the boys. My farming experience had given me the ability to puzzle through problems and meet the modern world head on. I learned that you're not a failure if you fail at one thing and I wanted my sons to understand that as well. Today, all three boys – you name it – they can fix it.

Jim attended Mt. Pleasant High School in Schenectady because they had better courses in math and science than Altamont. He graduated in 1962 and enrolled at the Maritime academy, which he had to leave because of a health problem that didn't allow him to stand at attention for long periods of time. After knocking about home for awhile he enlisted in the Air Force and became a very good airplane mechanic. He worked as a "turnaround man." Planes would come in from a mission and he turned them around, ready for another mission after any and all damage and repairs were made. While he was training I explained that all mechanical experience or dealings with fellow men were recorded in his mental library, which I pictured to him as the inside of a huge wheel. Whenever you're confronted with a problem, I told him, go to that wheel and with luck (or intelligence) you'll either find the answer or you'll find something to stimulate your mind to solve the problem.

While he was in Vietnam, Jim worked on a C130 where a bullet had pierced one of the gas tanks. The hole in the tank had to be patched, even though there was some fuel in the tank. On the top of the wing is a manhole big enough for a man to go in. Jim was the only one who volunteered. He set up a large fresh air pipe to blow air into the tank to mix with the fumes and give him enough air to breathe. To patch the hole he used an electric soldering iron inside so it wouldn't create a spark. He was able to solder a patch over the hole. He wasn't reckless. He anticipated problems and figured them out and received a Bronze Star for his service. He later wrote me that the mental library gave him the confidence he needed to solve the problem.

Ernie was a born farmer. I remember when we were camping in a private campground one summer, Ernie spent his time helping the neighboring farmer bring in his hay. While in college he had a business raising dairy replacement heifers. Farmers with larger herds don't have time to raise calves. This is how he paid for his two years of Ag School at Cobleskill, where he took regular down-to-earth farming and hydraulics. I don't know any of that stuff! Today Ernie has small acreage but he also rents other land and has 50 beef cattle and each year bales over 400 tons of hay for his own use and for sale. Some of the many happy years of my life were farming with Ernie. I bought an antique Lane sawmill and we restored it. We used his big Ford tractor to power the mill. I used the sawmill to cut the material for our 24 x 48-foot raised turkey building with slatted floor. We also cut lumber for the mill shed and, after Ernie left, I cut timbers and siding for several barns in

New Jersey.

Ernie decided to go into the construction business but was hampered by a lack of credit history. We cosigned a series of small notes, which he promptly repaid. With credit established, he was able to start building houses. His venture required a lot of capital and at one point the banks tightened up on credit, so even though he had never defaulted he couldn't continue in the building business. Being of good stock he didn't just curl up and die. Having experience in building he went to the banks and real estate people with run-down unsalable property and bargained like an expert to buy them as cheap as possible. It didn't matter the condition – he had the equipment and knowledge to turn them into rental income. He still has several properties as rental income. A few have been sold and he's been able to carry the mortgages. He's doing alright now and is not affected too much by the ups and downs of the economy. He's a diplomatic expert, able to collect rent on tough luck people. His son, Derik, is a partner in their business and Ernie now spends two months in Florida, where he also has a rental!

It seems Ernie and I took turns keeping each other on the straight path. One day he said, "Dad, I was offered a speedball, what should I do?" My mind raced to answer the question. After a brief pause I looked at him with loving but scared eyes. I chose to squeeze his bicep. "Son, God has given you a strong arm and a strong thigh. You have a strong straight body and if you think you'll be better off with a speedball and be liked any better only you can make that decision." I looked up and down at the length of his body, paused, and said "the decision is yours." For years I watched proudly as Ernie grew up and prospered, bought property, married, and had children. In some stories they all do live happily ever after.

When he wasn't in school, our youngest son, Ken, used to ride along with me to Cobleskill or Worcester when I was selling heavy road equipment. Ken was probably ten at the time and he was quiet and well behaved. He told me much later that he used to watch every move I made. He'd stand there and look around the machinery, listening to every word. "You know dad, when they would give you a reason for not doing something I was so impressed at how you turned it around in a good calm pleasant voice to overcome all those objections. I learned so much riding with you listening to you overcome objections." After graduating from high school in 1970, Ken worked for Wallace Armor Hardware in Schenectady. Though he did well there, he could see that his opportunities were limited due to the family nature of the business. When he was ready to marry, he asked Peg if she could help him get a job at Schenectady Chemical. Peg recalls that although they had openings, she waited for a good one. Eventually she spoke with a man who'd been transferred out to the research lab. He said, "I've been taking orders so long from people that I don't know how to give them. I hate using the telephone and I hate paperwork. If Ken wants this job he can have it tomorrow."

Ken took the job and loved it. At the time he was also becoming fascinated by computers, which were just coming out. Though I thought he was crazy for spending the money, he bought several early models and was able to use the knowledge he gained on his home computers to convince Schenectady Chemical to computerize their maintenance records. Since then he has worked for several large multi-million dollar companies and has done business in all the major countries of the world.

Today Ken works directly for one of his previous corporate clients and commutes from his home office in Altamont to New Jersey. In whatever spare time he has he works with his son Tim and restores the old machinery among other projects on the farm, like raising naturally grown turkey and pork with a progressive eye on growing natural grown vegetables and fruits. I'm grateful that Ken is there to keep an eye on me and Peg and I'm proud of what he's accomplished, though I worry about the stress in his life and hope that the farming will help him reconnect to his roots.

As a girl, Mary Jane spent her time on the side of the line Peg described that included house and garden and excluded barns and fields. Creative, resourceful, and full of life, she was never too interested in farming. With Peg working, she was pulled into watching her younger brothers after school. Peg remembers once, getting a call at work from Mary Jane that Ken had been bitten by a snake. Mary Jane took him down to Dr. Benjamin, whose wife was the school nurse. Mrs. Benjamin reassured her that the snakes around here were not poisonous, but that Ken shouldn't be playing with snakes in the future. In her free time, Mary Jane volunteered as a candy striper and decided to go to Wagner College on Staten Island for nursing, but then switched to sociology.

With years of 4-H and lifetime of country living, Mary Jane worked for the cooperative extension at Ballston Spa and was responsible for bringing in many new ways to do things. Forty years ago she founded Saratoga Suds, a handmade soap business inspired by her life at Pleasant View Farm. Like her father, Mary Jane was fascinated by early crafts. Saratoga Suds updated historical soap-making techniques with all kinds of different colors and scents in different shapes and textures. Well known in the Saratoga area, the soaps are available at the Old Songs Festival, Saratoga Farmers Market and other specialty shops. She also has a passion for fiber arts and has learned to spin – traveling to fiber shows around the northeast.

Even though we worked a lot – and I was traveling for sales most of the week –we still had a good time with the kids. On the weekends everyone had to get up for a family breakfast (regardless of how late they came in the night before!) They often had their friends over, since there was always something going on at the farm. The boys helped me farm and every year we made a point to go camping as a family to Cape Cod, the Catskills and Lewey Lake, along with many rides into Vermont and other beautiful places in the northeast. Today I'm so proud to see my children living full and honest lives. I realize that

I have often been insensitive and critical and need to see them as they are and not how I might want them to be. Each of our four children is the captain of their own ship of life and by now they know how to reach the port of their dreams. Good sailing to all our children, grandchildren, great grandchildren, and now great great grandchildren.

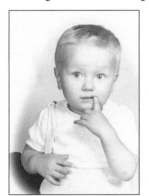   

Top: Ken, Ernie, Mary Jane, Jim
Lower photo taken October 2015. *Top row:* Ken, Ernie, Mary Jane, Jim. Bottom Row: Peg and Ev.

Longtime good friend, Ralph Hull, with Ev in the Grange Building at the Altamont Fair, 2006. Ralph is demonstrating a bee skip, made with rye straw. These were used to collect honey before modern bee hives. Ralph's book, *A life of Experiences and Memories,* was an inspiration to Ev.

Chapter 11

Community

Even when we were working long hours, on or off the farm, we tried to find time for our community. From the earliest days of our marriage we took on leadership roles in the Giffords Grange. As the kids moved on and Peg retired in 1988, my other activities multiplied. The greatest gift of volunteering is to feel the gratitude of so many people. At a recent Altamont Fair meeting Tom Della Rocco said his mother had been a member of the 4H Club that Peg and I led back in the forties.

The Grange

"The Grange was conceived and brought into being to stimulate rural people, both farm and non-farm, and to dignify as well as lighten their labor by diffusing knowledge and expanding the human mind." From The Grange 1867-1967: First Century of Service and Evolution

One of the tangible benefits of the Grange for farmers developed when the Grange League Federation formed a cooperative with the Dairymen's League to help small farmers purchase seed and other supplies at bulk prices. They combined members' orders for seeds, supplies – everything – and got wholesale prices for members. Eventually the cooperative morphed into Agway. Along with that grew something else. Good people were at the Grange meetings and when the local government started doing something they didn't like, they were a cohesive group and were able to have their voices heard. Then of course when good folks get together you've got to have a party. Birthdays. Easter. Christmas. A dance. Are we a little short of money? Let's put on a dinner. There was always something going on down at the Giffords Grange Hall at Route 397 and Route 20. We would put on dinners that wouldn't quit. We would always sell out. My wife and I benefited so much from the organization. Originally we were just members but we presented ourselves in such a way that we became leaders. You wear a different pair of glasses when you become a leader than when you're just sitting in one of the seats watching. Life takes a different meaning.

We always had a community service project in the works. One of my favorites was the Rocking Bed Project in the early fifties. Back then, before the Salk vaccine, polio was a terrible problem. We all knew people who had been stricken with polio, and there were many whose breathing was paralyzed too. They had to stay in iron lung machines. The March of Dimes started fundraising to help move people off of iron lungs and into rocking beds, which helped their lungs work and gave them more freedom of movement. The Pomona, or regional, grange decided that all the local granges would fundraise to purchase rocking beds for local hospitals. My wife and I were general chairmen of the campaign and we kicked the project off on May 1951, with an on-air fundraiser hosted by Earl Pudney and Bill Carpenter on WGY. It included leaders from Schoharie and Schenectady County granges. By the time the program ended in 1954 we had raised about $4,000, which was enough to buy three rocking beds and a page-turner for Ellis Hospital. To put that in perspective, you could buy a new car for under $1,000 in 1951!

Peg and I were at the Giffords Grange Hall in 1977 when they burned the paid-off mortgage for the building on a great big platter. At the time, Peg and I both wanted a modern toilet put in. We were the younger members and though several of us suggested that a flush toilet wouldn't cost that much, the older members didn't want to go back into debt. Unfortunately that split the membership, which we believe caused Gifford's Grange to close. A few of us joined the Glenville Grange. While my wife was secretary, we were attempting to collect delinquent dues. One of the members got a little up in the air and called us on the phone and spoke to my wife so rudely that we quit and went with the Hiawatha grange near Clarksville.

For Peg, the Grange was a source of personal strength and built her confidence. "Meeting me today you would never know I used to be bashful. I was teased by the other kids because I didn't have a mother – just a grandmother – and I never had the right clothes. At home I was constantly criticized by my stepmother and always felt very inferior. But when I became the lecturer for the grange, I became responsible for putting the program on each week. Then I'd have to speak for the grange at meetings if the senior member wasn't there. I got over my shyness because I had to. Ev and I both served in most of the Grange seats, including Master. We're still members but age has slowed us down and we can only contribute now as our condition allows."

AMWAY

"Life is hard by the yard. Inch by inch it's a cinch."
While experiences in The Grange built character, Amway developed positive thinking. Working with Tony and Sue Renard, we were exposed to attempting to sell an idea. Sometimes we believed 100% and if we didn't, we faked it. We loved their products and though I believe we spent more money on their nutritional supplements than we made, the expe-

rience was good for us because it built character and inner strength.

According to Peg, "Amway was very active in promoting Christianity. We saw more people there who came to know the Lord than anywhere else. If we were at a regional meeting in North Carolina on Sunday we would have our own church service. They asked for people to come forward and one time I was led up to the altar by a nice young man from Utica, named Little Tony Tefel. I've heard that poo-pooed many times by people who don't understand what it means – that you're changing your way of life because you've become a different person. One girlfriend said, 'I've been both sides of the coin and I like the way I am now better.' She didn't believe in anything. You can't be in the middle of the road. I feel that being a Christian, I'm on a train. My train is going down the track. If something causes my train to derail I know how to get back on the track. Something in your life leads you one way or another and makes you stay on track."

I noticed a change in Peg after she became born again. We both agree that we were defensive because of our childhoods. She often felt the need to strike back. After she was led to the altar where she made a vow, Lord forgive my sins, she changed. It wasn't an earthquake change, but more like her charisma. One day she was on the defensive, the next she was softer. More forgiving.

Ev Rau, Agricultural Historian

I've been involved with the Altamont Fair for most of my life. I was a member of 4-H and exhibited there as a teenager and my kids all participated. The fair has a large governing board and I've spent more than fifty years volunteering and in leadership roles, where I've made countless friends. My largest contribution has been in the antique machinery building, where I know how to run all the old machines that were used before gasoline power. And if I don't know how to run one, I know how to figure it out.

Several years ago, the fair sent out a brochure. They were planning a dinner and wanted me to set up a table with antique tools on it. I put a number by each tool and supplied a sheet of paper with numbers and everyone was supposed to guess what the tools were used for. The dinner was by invitation only and when Peg and I walked in, Ken, Sarah, and Pat along with Kristen and Tim were sitting at our table. I knew they weren't members and I whispered, "This is by invitation only." They didn't budge, but I remained concerned that someone would come to claim the seats. The program started and I announced who had guessed the tools, we handed out the prizes, and when I sat down, Peg whispered, "They want you back up there." The president, Joe Santorelli and Marie Mc-Millan made a little speech and handed me a plaque recognizing my role as Agricultural Historian to the Altamont Fair. I was taken completely by surprise. After taking a deep breath, I thanked everyone for the honor but also thanked everyone for all their work on the exhibits – especially the antique farm machinery museum. I told them, "Give yourself a hand." Of course I like the honor, but I only achieved what I did because of them.

One of the great things about working with the old equipment is training people, like Andy Tinning, who catch the same disease I have. He was very fortunate to find an old horse-drawn road scraper. It's a four-wheel thing with a blade that raises and lowers and tips. Back in the old days, the roads were paved with shale and gravel, and by spring

a lot of that material would be in the ditch. They'd have to reach over and bring it up and level it out. Carriage travel was getting so abundant that they needed to have good roads.

Andy called me one day and said that the wheels on the road scraper were rusted tight and wouldn't turn. I suggested that he jack up one wheel and get a 4x4 (piece of wood) and a small chain. With the wheel on an axel up in the air, we chained the 4x4 onto one of the wheel spokes. But after putting pressure on the 4x4, even with tremendous torque, the wheel was still stuck. We put the 4x4 in the other way and the wheel broke loose and turned! Archimedes said, Give me a place to stand and a lever and I will move the earth. I learned that in high school and it stuck with me. If the little short wrench doesn't do it, put a pipe on it and you'll triple and quadruple your strength.

Some of my happy moments accrued during the fair. If I saw a family looking at, say, the reaper and binder, it's easy to talk to them about the history of that machine and the labor saving and the next machine to replace it. My reward was to have the father of the young wide-eyed children extend a warm hand into mine and thank me sincerely for explaining the machine to his family.

Guilderland Historical Society

I joined the Guilderland Historical Society in the 1980s. After listening to the wisdom of old folks all my life, I began to realize that history was disappearing before my eyes and I was finally in a position to help preserve some of it. They were thrilled to learn the story of my great uncle Clayton, who went west to the gold mines and became a U.S. Marshall. He was shot in the line of duty and his badge and story are on display at the Society.

Over the years I met some good people in the historical society – Roger Keenholz, Mary Ellen Johnson, Mark Hessler, the Friebels, Alice Begley, Ruth Aberle, and many more. I used to enjoy the lectures and was happy to be able to contribute stories from the good old days and help with identifying photos and farm-related artifacts. I served as president for awhile and I think my biggest accomplishment was encouraging them to get a photocopier. We had these great pictures and it seemed like we should copy them and preserve them for the future. I liked the machine so much that we bought one for the house and that crazy machine is still working!

Dutch Barn Preservation Society

Mark Hessler was a member of the Guilderland Historical Society and took over as president in 1988 or 89. He was also a member of the Dutch Barn Preservation Society, which was founded in 1985. One day he said, "Ev, you have a Dutch barn, you should be a member of the DBPS." It took me about a year to act on that, but when I started going to meetings I loved it! I took on a number of roles and eventually became president. I learned so much about timber framing from the other members and from observing so many barns that I was asked to speak at historical societies all over the area, including Albany, Schuylerville, Knox, Duanesburg, and Schoharie Crossing. I would always donate my speaking fees to the DBPS even though we certainly could have used the extra money on the farm. Somehow or another you cast your bread on the water and it comes back to you.

The membership included artists, historians, farmers, and businessmen. I just enjoyed spending time with so many intelligent people of different professions who joined in their thinking to focus on one thing together. One of the most interesting people I met through the society was Dr. Vincent Shaeffer, who became a mentor and one of my best friends. Vince was a prominent scientist who invented cloud seeding and developed a nontoxic smoke bomb during World War II that was used to shield the ground from the enemy airplanes. In fact, they first tested it from Vrooman's Nose in Schoharie. One day he took me downstairs into his basement and opened his freezer and made it snow. It's the best way to understand cloud seeding, he laughed.

Being from Schenectady, Vince recognized the unique role that Dutch barns played as a bridge between the agricultural and architectural techniques of the old world and the lives of early settlers. He was unique because he was able to connect his passion for history with scientific discipline, clear writing, and mechanical insight to study and protect the barns, which were rapidly disappearing from the landscape. There's something about my mind that allows me to visualize all the different joinery I've ever seen in Vince's newsletters, in timber framing books, and in the barns I've visited. My practical knowledge, combined with Vince's scientific approach, allowed us to solve some really challenging restoration problems.

Just before I joined, the prominent local businessman and philanthropist Carl Touhey (aided and abetted by my good friend Vincent Shaeffer) arranged to have the larger of two Wemp barns moved from Schoharie Crossing to his place in Feura Bush for preservation. I got in on it after the timbers were there, and was in charge of the dedication of the building in 1990. There were at least 300 people at the event. I got together with Bill Freuh, whose hobby was Revolutionary War reenacting. He and his guys were in the crowd, milling about during the dedication. They had arranged to have three Tories, dressed differently, off in the brush. I had three balloons in my hand, and when I spoke about the barn and its roots in the Revolutionary War era, I said, wouldn't it be great to be there right now. When I let the balloons go, the drums started and there was a call to arms, which sent those guys over. Muskets were fired. The Tories were captured and their hands were tied. Then we had a barn dance and lots of great food including venison stew, which we prepared with the help of the Mayor of Altamont, Paul DeSorbo, in the old fashioned way.

The last project with Dr. Vincent Shaeffer was building a hay barracks for the Touhey farm. He had been researching Dutch hay barracks. These structures were used to protect hay before a barn was built or if the barn was full of drying grain. There were four-post, five-post or six-post structures with a thatched roof. There were holes in the supporting posts with wooden pegs so you could raise and lower the roof with pry bars as the level of hay changed. Although these temporary structures have all now disappeared, they were an important part of farming life in the eighteenth century. In our work on Dutch barns we had found posts from old hay barracks that were incorporated into more

Peter Sinclair, Keith Cramer, Ev Rau taken by Carl Touhey after moving his horse shed.

permanent structures. Vince built a model of one, based on his research, and asked if I thought I could build it. Of course I said yes.

The society came over and got oak trees off of my farm and hand hewed them. We had a drilling day. We used one of those drills where you sit on it and turn a crank. Not too many people could go too long because it's hard to do. You had to have holes a foot apart. On raising day we built the framework for the roof. I grew the rye straw for thatch while a good friend of mine, Mr. Kauffman from Kingston, did research and we learned how to thatch it. I now have a set of tools for thatching! Later, I was instrumental, through the Dutch Barn Society, in getting one of those historical signs made for the site. Sadly we had the dedication of the marker after Vince passed away. He was such a force that I'm not sure the society has ever fully recovered.

One memorable project involved a big barn down at Coeymans, owned by Paul Lawler. My grandson Tim and Paul's sons worked the timbers up. All the bents (timber frames shaped like a capital H) were raised with a machine except for the last one. There wasn't the right grade at that part of the site for a machine to raise it all the way up and Paul asked if we could raise it by hand. The bent was huge. The anchor beams were 12x24 inches. The ground dropped off, so the sill was about eight feet high at the low point of the hill. The skid steer lifted the bent up just a little bit above the sill level.

Raising day we had about six men and eight or nine women – some middle aged. Seeing them standing there, next to the bent, was a moment of reality for me. Everything was in order. We had two three-pulley block and tackles. The number of ropes in a block and tackle is the multiplication factor, so we had a multiplication factor of 12. I divided the men and women up. I had averaged their weights in my mind by multiplying 120 lbs by 14. It's close, I thought. They could pull that much before they skidded. I stood in the center and said, "I am the boss. This will only work if we work together. I will make you work together. I'll give you hand signals. When I say 'heave ho,' that means pull. If you see my hand clasp, hold it." I held my breath and the big thing came up slowly, but surely. I would have drowned myself it hadn't gone right.

When you raise a barn you see gravity at work. Think of a timber that weighs 1,000 pounds. If you have a scale on each side they're equal. As the timber rises it gets heavier near the ground and lighter on the top. In fact, you have to be careful as it gets toward vertical not to pull too far or it will topple over backwards. It is so hard in the beginning. When I say, "pull and hold," you have to do it. Because otherwise people could get hurt. Once it got close to vertical it was a piece of cake. At that point, Tim climbed to the top, reached up, put the peg in, and I was able to exhale. The old folks used the three words: observation, common sense, and reasoning. I was so proud. Paul was so grateful that he donated to the Dutch Barn Preservation Society, who eventually gave me a grant to buy the timbers to restore my Dutch barn.

Mabee Farm

My work with the Mabee farm began when they were soliciting bids to repair and move a building from an adjoining property. The building had belonged to the original Bradt family and was being given to the Mabee farm at no charge if they could move it. Though it was in pretty good shape, the west sill was completely gone and the north sill was questionable. The highest bid was 23,000 dollars and the lowest bid was 10,000. After reading the specs and seeing pictures, I told them that I knew how to save them 9,000 dollars. "I have the knowledge if you have four or five volunteers, want to buy a little lumber, and can get the town bulldozer. We'll move the building over here where you want it."

After replacing the west sill, we ordered two hemlock trees about 20 inches in diameter and 25 feet long. The building was up on a rickety stone foundation. We placed two skids under the building with X-braces and a compression timber for the two skids. We diagonally braced the walls, which kept the small building from being damaged from the stresses of moving over uneven ground. The building had to make four 90-degree

turns. It was pulled by the bulldozer and skidded on the hemlock trees, like ski runners. We had four people – one on each corner. I was off to the side and I instructed them to holler if they saw anything amiss. They pulled it 10 feet to test while I watched. The ground was basically level, though not 100 percent. It went perfect. The bulldozer moved slowly while we watched. After the chains were tight, I rechecked everything and told them to take it over. Guys walked near the four corners all the way over. There were stakes where they wanted it to go and we just moved it into place.

Later we heard about a Dutch barn up around Fultonville that was going to come down because they were making a golf course. I rode up with Keith Cramer, John van Schoick, and a couple of others. We took a video and they asked me to appraise the building. We noticed old water stains and I could see that water had been running down the timbers going into the joints. As a result there was some shifting of the timbers. Unfortunately, due to a measurement error, the old building did not quite fit the new foundation. One day I was in the completed building after a thunderstorm when the wind was blowing hard and I saw that the main gable end was oil canning. You can have a little movement on a pin frame building but you can't have the whole side going in and out or the building will have a problem. I donated some cable and we drilled holes through the big timbers and added a huge turnbuckle, which stopped the walls from going in and out with the wind.

The year after the big Dutch barn was open for visitors, the committee was asked to find a community project for training local Seabees. I suggested building a carriage shed and made a scale model. Once we had the stone foundation in place, I ordered lumber from Rudy Stemple's saw mill in East Berne and the 20-foot hemlock roof rafters came from the tall clear trees from my woods. The lumber was delivered to the Mabee site and 40 Seabees set about learning how to do timber framing. It was probably the most mind-challenging project of my life because of size of the crew. But the sound of so many saws, mallets, and chisels was music to my ears as the crew worked to assemble the walls and end sections while waiting for a backhoe to lift the frame. The officer in charge coaxed me into putting up one section in the old way, so we rigged the block and tackle and raised it up. When all the sections were pinned in place and the roof rafters were spiked in position, the Seabees' training was complete and a monument to teamwork.

Future buildings included a blacksmith shop for the resident blacksmith, John Ackner, a carpenter shop, and a corn crib. Later, when I was working with some volunteers on the new blacksmith shop I heard the trustees complain about the price of the lumber. I suggested that they advertise in the newspaper and sell timber-framing classes with a fee for each person per weekend. It took three weekends to erect a structure and the fees helped buy lumber. I knew that if people paid good money they should get recognition, so I publicly commended each one when they did anything right. Those buildings went up so fast and so well and I built friendships that wouldn't quit. One of the students said, "You know I paid more money for another class, but I learned a lot more from you." I think this was because I carefully observed each person and we worked as a team.

Top left: Raising the carpenter shop "the old way." *Top right*: Blacksmith shop with carpenter shop in background.
Middle right: Carpenter shop.
Below left: Demonstration of hand flailing at a Mabee Farm event. *Bottom righ*t: Ev demonstrating antique tools.

Hip Hip Huzza!

As a Mabee Farm volunteer I was often called to explain early pioneer life to the fourth and seventh graders who came through on field trips. I focused on vegetables and farming in the early 1700s. My most successful presentation was a demonstration of hand flailing and winnowing grain. It was an emotional moment for me, seeing young people take the flail in hand and actually flail the grain by themselves as they connected with a thousand-year-old skill. No one was criticized and each one was praised for participating, even if a master hand helped them along.

I recall reading once in a National Geographic magazine that the hull of the Revolutionary war battleship, Old Ironsides, was 24" thick, but not solid. It was made of many different layers. This made the outside so strong that when British cannonballs hit they would bounce off. The sailors would cheer *Hip Hip Huzza!* with each failed strike. At the Mabee Farm there was a huge willow stump near the parking lot. When three to four busloads of school kids were ready to leave I'd ask who wanted to help. We'd climb on the stump. We'd say *Hip Hip Huzzah* three times — first low, then loud and then, finally, really loud. Whenever I went to any historical society I'd finish my talk, ask for any questions, and then say, "Now I'd like you to help me with something." We'd all shout *Hip Hip Huzzah!* three times as thanks for inviting me. The Lord gave me a few commonsense ways to win friends and influence people. Of course, Dale Carnegie helped out a little too!

Community projects on Pleasant View Farm

Top: Harvesting grain with Kevin Stewart to be used on an 1865 Campbell threshing machine in an Altamont Fair demonstration project in 2007.

Bottom left: Oats being harvested for the Altamont Fair threshing exhibit.

Bottom right: Rye field harvested for the thatched roof of an authentic English carriage shed being constructed at Shakespeare & Company in Lenox, MA.

Dutch Barn Study Center

Being a member of the Dutch Barn Preservation Society, I was asked to consult with the Bell Top Elementary School in North Greenbush. They wanted to build a Dutch barn as a study center and were gathering information before they committed to spending thousands of dollars on timbers. In talking with the superintendent, the principal, and couple of teachers, I suggested that instead of just a Dutch barn, that they make a Dutch barn on one end and an English barn on the other. I didn't have any idea how to do it, but they were excited by the idea so I offered to figure it out.

Once the barn was up they had a dedication. They arranged to have a horse and an old-fashioned cart. My wife sat up front and I sat in the back. I'll never forget how proud I was to have my wife and myself brought in that way. I secretly arranged for another stunt with Bill Frueh, the Revolutionary War reenactor. I had a couple of balloons. At a given time when the program was over, I let go of the balloons. The reenactors had been hiding behind the corner of the school. When they saw the balloons they started beating the drums and marched around the corner with their muskets. They must have enjoyed the show because when they celebrated their 10th anniversary they invited me back again. So grateful to Mr. Ferris, Melanie, Chris, Brian McDonald, Ken Bailey, and all the others.

Dutch Barn Society Teaching Model

The Dutch Barn Society got a grant to make a 1/4 scale model barn that goes into the high schools to use as a building training project. They made it accurately. Put it together. Took it apart. Three months later they were all set to put it up at the Altamont Fair. It was on the program. But it didn't work. The tenons wouldn't go in. We realized that when timber framing you work with green lumber and the tenon, being one-inch thick will shrink less than the 3x4 inch beam. You put the tenon in there and later the beam shrinks around it and holds it tight. The pin holds it but nature cooperates and shrinks the big piece around the smaller piece. Since we had taken the model apart and let it sit for three months, the beam continued to shrink and the tenon was now too large to fit into the mortise. Luckily one of the guys brought his tools along and we spent about an hour shaving the tenons down. Then a month later they had to be shaved again!!

While we were there working on the model barn a young woman came up to me and tapped me on the shoulder. She asked if it was possible for her little boy to be involved in the project somehow. I looked at her and she was so emotionally sincere. I took it that the husband was gone. She was being the mother and the father. I had the little boy help me with the wall braces and told him what to do, how to hold his hands and put the braces up. When we were finished I watched him go to his mother. She came over with her eyes glistening, holding back the tears, and thanked me for letting her little boy help put the barn up. I never saw them again, but I carry those memories in my heart.

Keepsakes from a life of service
Peg's certificate of community service from 4-H.
Dr. Vincent Shaeffer with Ev and Peg on their 50th wedding anniversary.
Building the demonstration barn at Bell Top
Commemorative pins from the Mabee Farm and the Grange.

Ev holding up his model to show how the new barn will look in the landscape. 2007.

Chapter 12

Building our Barn

Sometime in 2006 I noticed that the sheep had grazed the grass so I could see some of the foundation stones of our original German threshing barn. I was showing my youngest son, Ken, and his son Tim. The barn had been built prior to 1800 and I can remember as a young child, playing inside with puppies, that even then it was leaning and sagging. It finally came down in 1930. It takes 20 to 40 years to bring a barn down after the roof starts to leak, so it must have been neglected for a very long time. This one was a typical German threshing barn – 26x42 feet. We had old photos of it next to the Dutch barn so we knew that there had always been three barns and we had a good idea of how the foundation was oriented, because the large corner stones had moved very little over 120 years. They said, "Why don't we rebuild it!" By then I had been involved in a number of barn projects. Ken and Tim had been involved in some of them and had long heard me lament the missing barn.

The more we talked, the more the idea took hold. In 2006 we walked the farm and identified timber trees that we could use for lumber. We needed white pine and hemlock trees, 18-30 inches diameter. Rudy Stemple of Berne agreed to buy the trees and cut timbers and siding for us. He was surprised I could give him an exact lumber list out of my head but after working on so many projects with the Dutch Barn Society I could do it today. I know what it takes to build a barn!

In the spring of 2007, while waiting for the lumber, we poured new concrete piers. Unfortunately the cornerstones had settled a little over the years, so we made forms to the level of the old corner stones and poured concrete for the four corners and formed twelve other piers to support the main floor timbers. With the corners established, we ordered the sills. These timbers would be 10x12 inches by 22 feet long and the green wood would weigh over 1,000 pounds. Once the sills arrived in 2007, our good friends Pat and Gerard Marciano came with their team of big beautiful draft horses and easily skidded the sills into place.

The final barn would be 26x42 feet, so the 22-foot sill timbers needed to be half lapped. Once the timbers arrived, we began the tedious and exacting work of half lapping the sills and mortising and tenoning the cross timbers and smaller floor timbers. To make a mortise by hand, you use a stationary drill with a hand crank. All mortises are two inches wide, so you drill three holes and take a two-inch chisel and mallet and remove the excess wood. Rather than put the plank floor down immediately, we used the floor timbers as big flat saw horses when we made the bents. A bent is shaped like a capital H and four bents create the structure of the barn. Once the bents are finished, you measure and fit the wall plates (which were notched before raising) for the siding studs.

My grandson Tim was the main worker on the crew and I would awaken every morning to the sound of his hammer and chisel at 5:30 a.m. He had graduated from Hudson Valley in a technical program and was initially skeptical about the old building techniques. His first traditional project was the Pleasant View Farm sign! While making the sign posts and later, while building the barn, it could get a little comical when Tim and I disagreed on how to do things. He came green, unfamiliar with that work, but educated in contemporary building techniques which sometimes contradicted the older ways. You've got a 12x12-inch timber and you want a 2x6-inch wide mortise. It better be accurate, but it doesn't have to be perfect. I can't tell you how many times I said, "Come on, you're not building a china closet. You're building a barn!" Nevertheless he absorbed many of the ideas that he uses today as a qualified barn wright.

Our friend Chuck Dziegiel was hunting turkeys that spring and when he heard about the barn, suggested that I call his friend Kirk Greenfield. Kirk had been a steelworker and also worked with lath and plaster. He was so impressed when I handed him a mallet and chisel and explained how to make the joints, that he spent the rest of the summer working with Ken, Tim and the other volunteers on the timbers, using a hand saw and a two-inch mortising drill. They spent many hours assembling all the matching sections on the floor deck to check and recheck that all connecting joints were perfect for Raising Day.

The Pleasant View Farm sign was made from an old photo of my uncle Willard Ogsbury delivering eggs, raw milk, and farm produce from a wagon in Altamont. Our son, Ken, and our granddaughter Meredith, had the picture duplicated and carved on wood and painted. Tim and I worked together on the frame.

Rudy Stemple milled locust posts for the sign, which need no preservatives, and Tim made mortise and tenon joints. The trick with mortise and tenon is that you don't line up the holes exactly – and you use a draw pin, which draws the wood in tight and permanent at the joints.

Kirk Greenfield (left) using a hand-crank mortising drill to make a mortise. Grandson Tim (right) using a curved adz to smooth a half lap.

Raising Day

It was a beautiful October day in 2007 with the sun at high noon, setting the stage for the biggest barn project of my life. Excitement ran through Ken, Tim, and me. The rafters, siding, and roofing were at the barn site. Fifty or more people came from all over – some total strangers. Some came to help and many to watch. There were cars all over and we set up lumber benches in the field. Those who put in the physical power got to experience the lifestyle of Grandfather Peter Ogsbury, the Civil War veteran.

The barn raising was Tim's first big project and when the first timber frame went up, he stood back and said, "Grandpa it's so tall!" Today Tim's an expert in Dutch barn construction and travels around the country restoring and reconstructing historic barns. He can look at a field full of unmarked timbers and know exactly where they go. He thinks and acts like the barn builders of long ago, but he uses all the up-to-date power tools. Peg and I are proud to see Tim with a successful and profitable trade. After a recent trip I told him, "You're no longer a laborer. You're a master craftsman. You do not have to dance to someone else's drum."

When you have 20 to 40 people working on a job site, I've learned that there can be only one boss if you're going to keep everyone safe. I told everyone that I was the only boss and the most important thing that day was that no one got hurt. "If the barn goes up today, that will be an added benefit." We had timbers on sawhorses, building the frames on the ground before raising them up. There was one guy showing off his strength and as he swung a piece of timber around he managed to hit me. I called out STOP and there was complete silence. I was probably too loud, but I had to make a point. I told him to slow down, walked over and shook his hand and smiled. He did work at a slower pace.

Raising the bents takes discipline, a block and tackle, and about 25 people pulling together. What's interesting is that as you're starting to lift the bent, you're pulling up 50% of its weight. But as the bent lifts, the amount of weight decreases. Once it comes up over about 45 degrees, it becomes easier to manage until it gets to vertical, when one person could maneuver it. At that point we have someone pulling from the other side to make sure it doesn't tip over in the other direction. When the second bent is erected, a "girt" or cross piece is added and the structure, held in place with a one-inch hardwood pin, becomes rock solid. After the first timber, the later ones become routine. We were done before dark. It was a good day for all.

I believe in a greater power. Putting a barn up the old fashioned way is a dangerous business and we had total strangers here. Through many sleepless nights, I had put that barn up and down so many times in my head that when it went up, it went up absolutely perfectly. It went just the way I had put it up a dozen times while tossing and turning in bed. Not a single thing happened that day that I had not thought about beforehand.

That year we finished the basic frame – a rigid frame box. The roof wouldn't be put on until the following year (2008) and you need the roof to protect the joints from water infiltration, so my son Ken, who's a perfectionist too, climbed over the structure and painted every joint with wood preservative to protect them from the elements. In 2008 we added the roof rafters, roof boards, siding, and doors using the original wrought iron hinges from the old barn.

One of my Dutch Barn Society members, Peter Sinclair, had suffered a stroke on his right side, which meant that he had to become left handed. A young lady named Roberta Jeracka called me and asked if Peter could come up and see us working on the Barn. Did I think he could do something to be a part of the project? By then the barn was built but the siding was not on yet. We needed to put window frames in before the siding. To do that, we would cut a slot into two facing wall studs to slide in a 2x8, which would be the window sill. I realized that making the slots would be a perfect project for Peter. He came with his tools. He had one hand and I had two. We drew a pencil line and we had to saw that. We sawed two notches about 3/8 inch deep on the opposing studs. Then we used a chisel to take out wood and make a groove. Peter and I took turns. He would hold the chisel. I would take the mallet. I would hold the chisel. He would take the mallet. We made the two grooves for that window sill to slide in. That will always be Peter's window.

When we finished the barn in November 2008, we hosted a Thanksgiving dinner for 45 people. Though air came up through the floor planks, the conditions were tolerable, so we persevered. Instead of setting one long table, we set the tables in a circle in the center of the barn with construction heaters inside the circle and food off to the side. When I rose to give thanks my heart was so overwhelmed by the kindness and generosity of so many people that I just cried like a baby. Kirk Greenfield said some nice words and some of my children spoke. When I pulled myself together I remembered Bill Hay from years past helping on the saw mill and Kirk volunteering for two summers in 2007 and 2008. And I was of course so grateful to have worked with Tim and Ken.

Looking back, it seems that my whole life had been directed toward this moment. My knowledge of timber framing came gradually from watching my father and brother use cables and turnbuckles. But it was by joining barn tours and observing different building styles and working and talking with friends like Jack Sobin in the Dutch Barn Preservation Society, that I was able to learn about old tools and timber framing from masters.

Upper left: Neighbor Ray Smith with Tim

Upper right: Tim and Ken

Middle: Fully sided barn

Lower left: Ev and Peg enjoying Thanksgiving dinner in the new barn with Ev's model as the centerpiece.

Chapter 13

Closing the Circle

2014 was the first year that I didn't carve the turkey at Thanksgiving. All Peg and I had to do was make some oyster dressing for about five people. There were over 30 people at my son Ernie's house. They managed to get us all into one room with a U-shaped table. Ernie was carving the turkey because when I stand for a long period of time I feel like there's a knife going through my back. When I said grace, I began to thank the Lord for everything and then I said, there's happiness and sadness in this day. It's happy that everyone is here together. But this is the first time I have not been able to carve the turkey for my family. I choked up and it was difficult to get my voice going again. I worked it through and finished grace.

When Ernie was finished carving, though he's not a public speaker, he clinked a glass to get everyone's attention. He must have recognized how difficult it was for me at that moment. He spoke to all and made a good point that the family was altogether and that was the most important thing. He mentioned that he goes to Florida for two months in the winter. He's met quite a few prosperous people who say they have plenty of money to fly their family down to be with them on the holiday but they won't come. We've got to thank God that we are all here together and it doesn't matter who carves the turkey. That took a lot of weight off of me. I'm so happy to have someone else to be able to rise to the occasion, realizing it wasn't easy for him – or for me.

Ninety-six years can go fast if you're busy. Seeing my son carve the turkey reminded me of the reality of my age and life. It's hard to recognize that someday I won't be here and Ernie and Ken will be doing it. We do today's job. It doesn't matter what the past is. A lot of people get off on the wrong road by their mind's own undoing of a good day. Still, I worry that our children are caught up in busy modern lives, connected by digital devices but not always connecting as people. I worry that while they're making good money they may not be living full lives.

I think of my grandfather sleeping soundly knowing that his daughter (my mother and father) would step in to run the farm and take care of him. Peg and I then farmed, kept the old homestead and took care of my mother and father. As the years have passed, we've dealt with many calamities with the help of our children. Between us we've faced congestive heart failure, broken hips, prostate cancer, irregular heartbeats, and creeping immobility. Though our children have been quick to react to each crisis with love and care, we sometimes worry about what will happen when just one of us is left behind at the homestead on the top of the hill.

On the bright side, there are signs of renewal and rebirth that give me hope that a new generation of farmers will discover the joys of a farming life – both in our family and in the world at large. A revolution is taking place in our understanding of the health benefits of food that comes from diversified farms. Doctors have long been aware that diet affects health. But now they are starting to see the relationship between healthy soil and a healthy body. Small family farms contribute to environmental sustainability while providing tastier food with higher nutritional content. Peg and I have long read books about food and health and we're thrilled that our children are taking up the challenge and educating themselves about progressive farming methods. This year we will have pastured turkeys and pigs, along with heirloom vegetables grown in the good old ways. The original Dutch barn that Peter Ogsbury moved from the Pangburn farm is being restored by my grandson, Tim, thanks to a grant from the Dutch Barn Preservation Society.

I feel like a ship on the sea of life. In my childhood I passed a pirate ship. I had problems but sailed on and welcomed on board my wife as my first mate. We were joined by a crew of friends and family who helped keep the ship sailing through childhood and the storms of life. Our good friend Kirk's wife, Sherry Greenfield, always says, "Get over it!" but as my book draws to a close I think a better phrase might be, "Let's get on with it!"

Ev with son Ken and grandson Tim with their heritage potatoes and corn in 2015.

In Gratitude

In bringing this book to a close, I realize there are many people who have made a lasting impression on my life, but who did not appear in the pages of my book. I hope I can be forgiven if important names escape me, but here are special thanks to some who have made a difference in my life.

Paul Harvey, in his book, *God Made a Farmer*, captured the spirit of devotion and love of the soil and animals that I have seen in so many of my farming friends: the Gade Farm Family, Peter Ten Eyck of Indian Ladder Farms, Richard & Shirley Ball and crew at the Carrot Barn, Carl Peterson, and the Abbruzzese family past and present.

My mind was nourished by the brilliant people I worked with at G.E., like Carl Seaward (and later his son Bill), and many wonderful people I've met in later life, like Professor Lou Ismay. I'm especially grateful to the historical societies, whose members are so stimulating:

• Mabee Farm Historic Site and volunteers, especially Kim and Gary Mabee, John Ackner, Win Biglow, Dale Wade-Keszey, and Mary Kuykendall Weber for pictures of the Mabee Farm
• The Altamont Fair officers, members, and associate members
• The Guilderland Historical Society
• Marijo Dougherty of the Altamont Archives and Museum
• Special thanks to Peter Sinclair of Hudson Valley Vernacular Architecture
• Michael Burrey from Plimouth Plantation

• The Dutch Barn Preservation Society and all the officers past and present including Keith Cramer, Ned Pratt, Skip Barshied, Vince Shaeffer, Thomas Lanni, Chris and Tim Albright

The churches have nourished my spirit. Thanks to the good people from St. John's Lutheran Church, especially the Men's Breakfast, Altamont Reformed Church, and St. Lucy's.

Thanks to the Town of Guilderland Road Crew, the volunteer fireman, the local police, county sheriff, and staff, and the Altamont Rescue Squad for taking such good care of our family.

Thanks to the Altamont Enterprise and other local papers for telling our stories.

Thanks to Robert Ritchie, his son, and my graduating class from Altamont High School. And to our good neighbors – near, far, and long gone – Ray Smith and John Hughes, the Lainhart family, the Stewart family, Bill Brehm and Beverly Brehm White, Mike and Pat Davis, Don, Devin, Tina Lamb, the LeClairs, the Fredericks, the Butlers, the Basslers, and the Baldauf family past and present. And thanks to all the children of our dear friends who have become part of our life today.

Thanks to Joyce Barber Vedder for her many kindesses.

Thanks to Laura Shore for her good humor and infinite patience in bringing this story to life.

— *Everett W. Rau 2015*

Memorial

As work on this book was coming to a close
we learned of the untimely passing of our dear friend
Mark Burlingame.
I will always see Burls in the morning sunrise
and in the mysteries of the beautiful shadows at the end
of the day and whisper, silently, to God
the question "Why?"

This book is dedicated to Mark's son, Jason,
who has become a friend of the family
through his close friendship with our grandson Tim.